FIRST
FUN
SCIENCE
ENCYCLOPEDIA

First published in 2002 by
Miles Kelly Publishing Ltd
Bardfield Centre
Great Bardfield
Essex CM7 4SL

2 4 6 8 10 9 7 5 3 1

British Library Cataloguing-in-Publication Data
A catalogue record for this book is available from the British Library

ISBN 1-84236-163-5

Printed in Hong Kong

Author
Brian Ward

Project Editor
Amanda Learmonth

Assistant Editor
Nicola Sail

Copy Editor
Ann Kay

Design
WhiteLight

Design Assistant
Maya Currell

Picture Research
Bethany Walker

Proofreader
Lynn Bresler

Index
Jane Parker

Consultant
Steve Parker

www.mileskelly.net
info@mileskelly.net

FIRST FUN SCIENCE ENCYCLOPEDIA

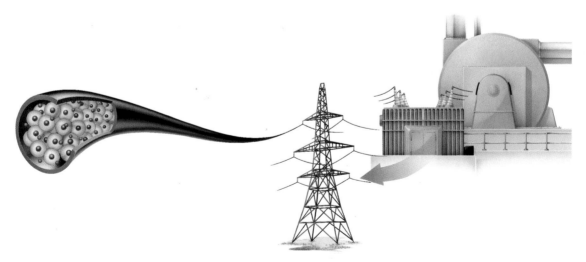

Brian Ward

Miles Kelly

PUBLISHING

Contents

How to use this book

Your *First Fun Science Encyclopedia* is bursting with information, colour pictures and fun experiments to do. The pages run from A to Z with a new subject on every page. This will help you find information quickly and easily. There are comic cartoons to bring amazing true facts to life and puzzles and games to tease your brain. The index at the back of the book will help you look for specific information.

Colour bands
Your encyclopedia has six subject areas. The coloured bands along the top of each page tell you which subject area you are in.
• Technology has red bands.
• Energy, Forces and Motion has orange bands.
• Living World has green bands.
• Discovering Science has purple bands.
• Earth and Space has blue bands.
• Light, Sound and Electricity has yellow bands.

Activity and puzzle boxes
Some pages will have activities, games or puzzles for you to do. Look for the green or blue panels.

Word boxes
New or difficult words are explained in the yellow panels.

Alphabet strip
Your book is alphabetical. This means it runs from A to Z. Along the bottom of every page is an alphabet strip. The letter that starts the main heading is in bold. Above the letter there's a small arrow to highlight where you are in the alphabet.

6

Colour

Try this!
Have fun mixing lots of colours with your paints. Blue, yellow and red are the primary paint colours (these are different from the primary light colours – see 'Mixing light'). See how many different colours you can come up with. You'll be amazed!

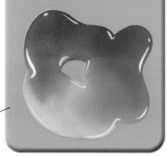

When we look at an object, we do no see its colour. Instead, we see the light that reflects, or bounces off. White light (a mix of a falls on the object, but most of its colours are a The colours that are reflected reach our eyes ar object its colour. So, we see a leaf as green bec absorbs all other coloured light except green.

◀ Natural colour
Flowers are brightly coloured to attract insects such as bees, which help to pollinate them (make them reproduce). Bees' eyes can see colours and patterns that are invisible to us.

◀ Mixing light
Red, green and blue are th colours of light. They co together to produce colour. When two mixed, they make colour. If equal am primary light colou together, they make

Word box
absorb
soak up

reproduce
when living things make more of their own kind

▲ The spec
Here, ordinary whi through a triangula called a prism. This into its different col range of bands of c spectrum. You can this effect when sun through a vase of v

6 a b **c** d e f g h i j k l m n o p q r s t u v

Main text
Every page begins with a paragraph of main text to each subject.

Cross-references
Within the colour band are cross-references to other subjects. These tell you where you can find more information about your chosen topic. Follow the arrows to turn backwards or forwards to the correct page.

Pictures
Illustrations or photographs accompany each caption. Many illustrations are labelled to explain what different parts of them are called.

Communication

Find out more:
Computers ▶ Internet ▶ Technology ▶

Our whole life is based on communication. We communicate when we speak or wave to someone, and when we send a letter. Modern technology allows us to communicate at very high speeds right across the world – by telephone, radio, television or the Internet.

▲ Internet phone

This mobile phone lets you make voice calls, browse the Internet and send text messages and emails. Some allow you to listen to the radio or even watch TV.

▶ Let's communicate!

As well as words, we use a lot of 'body language' to communicate with people – often to say hello or goodbye. Hand gestures, facial expressions, body positions and eye contact are all ways of communicating with others.

Wow!
One of the longest phone calls ever recorded lasted for 550 hours – nearly a whole month!

Captions
Captions give you detailed information about all the photographs and illustrations in your book.

Wow boxes
Look for the orange panels to read amazing true facts – the funny cartoons will make you laugh!

a b c d e f g h i j k l m n o p q r s t u v w x y z 7

Air

You can't see it, but you can't live without it! Air is all around us, and it contains the oxygen you need in order to live. Air also has weight, and it is pressing on you all of the time, although you won't be aware of it.

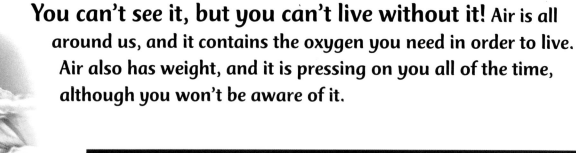

▲ Up in the clouds

The clear air over mountains is very thin and often difficult to breathe. This is because of the high altitude. Air is also much cooler at high altitudes. If wind pushes air up over high peaks, the air cools. The water in the air then 'condenses' to form clouds.

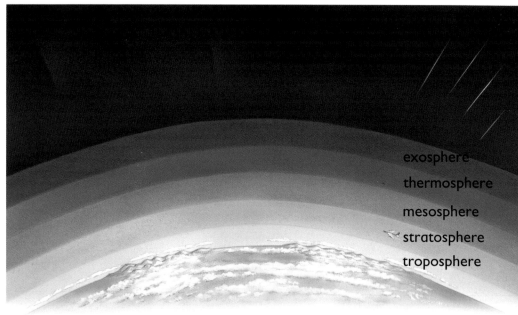

exosphere
thermosphere
mesosphere
stratosphere
troposphere

▼ Underwater air

Fish have special body parts, gills, to breathe the oxygen in water. We do not, so divers carry a cylinder of gases including oxygen on their backs, so that they can breathe underwater.

▲ Layers and layers of air

Although you can't see them, the air around the world is in layers like an onion. Jet airliners fly mostly in a layer called the stratosphere. Other air layers extend far out to space. Together, all the layers make up the Earth's 'atmosphere'.

Word box

altitude
height above the ground

oxygen
colourless gas in the air we breathe

stratosphere
part of the atmosphere

Aircraft

flap

rib

spar

Aircraft fly through the air, supported by their wings, and allow us to travel at high speeds to distant places. Aircraft are lifted into the air by the force of air flowing over their curved wings as their engines push them forwards.

aileron

tip

▲ On the wing

The wing of an aircraft is curved to provide lift. It is very strong but also light, because it is made of special alloys. Hinged flaps and ailerons can be moved to change the wing's shape and move the aircraft.

▲ Fighter planes

The Spitfire was a graceful fighter plane that played an important part in World War II. It became one of the fastest propeller-driven aircraft. It was replaced by newer jet-powered fighters.

► Jumbo jets

A modern 'Jumbo' jet can carry up to 500 passengers for thousands of kilometres without stopping for more fuel. These huge aircraft have two decks, like a ship. Their weight is supported by a complicated set of wheels.

Wow!
Some fighter aircraft can fly so fast that they could catch up with their own bullets!

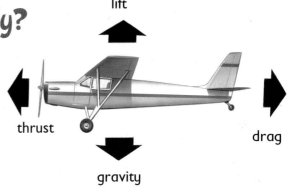

Word box

aileron
surface on a plane's wing used to control the plane's direction

alloy
a mixture of metals

► How does it fly?

Planes fly by balancing opposite forces. Gravity pulls the plane down, while lift pulls it up. Thrust propels the plane forwards, but drag, caused by air resistance, holds it back.

lift

thrust

drag

gravity

Animal kingdom

Find out more:
Animal life ▶ Birds ▶ Fish ▶ Insects and spiders ▶
Mammals ▶ Reptiles ▶

Animals are one of the two kingdoms of living things (the other is the plant kingdom). Animals can be so tiny that you need a microscope to see them, or as huge as a whale or an elephant.

◀ Insects

All insects have six legs when adult. Their bodies are divided into three sections: the head, thorax and abdomen. Many also have wings.

◀ Look – no legs!

Snakes are reptiles that once, long ago, had legs! They move by making wavelike movements with their muscular bodies. A snake's whole body is covered with protective scales.

▶ The Emperor

Birds are found across most of the world. This emperor penguin lives in the icy Antarctic. It walks for kilometres across ice to its breeding ground. Once in the water, it is a graceful and fast swimmer, hunting for fish.

▲ Fast mover

Fish live in all types of water, from deep oceans to streams and tiny pools. This sailfish is one of the fastest-swimming fish. It travels through the oceans in search of smaller fish to eat, slashing at them with its swordlike beak.

▼ Is it a fish?

This bottlenose whale is shaped like a fish, but it is a mammal, just like lions, elephants – and you! Over millions of years the whale's front legs have changed into flippers, to help it to swim.

Word box

amphibian
a cold-blooded animal that lives in water when young and on land when grown up

▶ Thin skin

Amphibians such as frogs have thin, delicate skin, which they must keep moist. Amphibians breed in water. They produce young called tadpoles or larvae ('larv-eee'), which look very different from the adults.

Animal life

Find out more:
Animal kingdom ◄ Birds ► Fish ► Insects and spiders ►
Mammals ► Reptiles ►

Animals are found in the ocean depths, the parched deserts, rocky mountains and even the icy North and South Poles. Different animals have bodies that have adapted to suit the places where they live.

► Rocky heights

Many sheep live in green fields on farms. Some, however, like this one, are wild mountain sheep. They live high up among the peaks, and can leap gracefully from rock to rock. This ram (male sheep) has large horns, which he uses to fight other rams.

▲ Having fun

Dolphins are small whales that are common around the world. These are very curious, clever and playful animals. Dolphins swim in large groups. They seem to enjoy leaping high out of the water, as well as following ships and boats.

◄ The open plains

Elephants are the world's largest land animals. The African savannah elephant is adapted to live on Africa's hot, grassy plains. It feeds on grass and leaves, which it pulls down with its long, flexible trunk. The Asian elephant is smaller and lives in thick jungle.

▼ Muddy mounds

Termites are antlike insects that live in many hot parts of the world. These ingenious insects build their homes from great mounds of mud. Inside are many 'rooms' and tunnels, where termites live in huge colonies (groups).

Wow!

The cheetah is the fastest land animal in the world. It can run up to 100 kilometres per hour – as fast as a car!

▲ Animal journeys

Snow geese, like many other birds, mammals and fish, migrate (travel) very long distances. This is usually done to find food, or to reach places where they can breed.

Astronomy

Do you like looking at the stars in the night sky? Astronomy is the study of these stars. It is also the study of our Moon, the planets in our Solar System and all kinds of objects found in the Universe. In ancient times, people studied the Moon's movements to make the first calendars. Now astronomers use amazing technology to see farther into space than ever before.

Make a star mural

Have stars twinkling on your own bedroom wall!
1. Cut out star shapes from shiny sweet wrappers. Glue the stars onto a large sheet of black paper.
2. Brush some PVA glue onto the paper and sprinkle glitter over it. Shake off any loose glitter.
3. Stick your star mural up on the wall with multi-purpose tac.

▶ Seeing by radio

The light from the stars you can see has taken millions of years to reach us. Some stars are so far away that we can't even see them. However, they produce faint radio waves that we can measure. Huge metal dishes called radio telescopes collect these radio waves. Some scientists think they have found radio waves left over from when the Universe began.

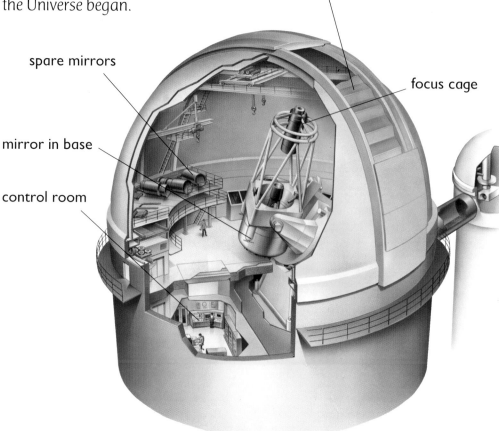

sliding roof

spare mirrors

focus cage

mirror in base

control room

▶ Watching the sky

Modern astronomers use huge telescopes with giant mirrors and lenses. These help them to see objects millions of kilometres away. The telescopes are kept in buildings called observatories. Parts of the roof slide back so that the telescope can be pointed at the sky. The telescope slowly moves around as the Earth turns, to watch the same patch of sky.

Atoms and molecules

Find out more:
Materials ▶ Solids, liquids and gases ▶
Water ▶

Atoms are some of the smallest objects that exist – so small that they are invisible. Everything around us is built from billions of them. Atoms do not usually exist on their own, but join together to make molecules. Two or more atoms joined are a molecule.

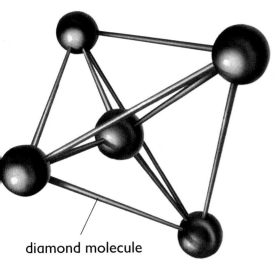

diamond molecule

▲ Coal or diamond?

It seems odd to compare a precious diamond with a lump of common coal, but they are, in fact, very similar! Both contain carbon atoms. In coal, the atoms of carbon are joined up in one particular way. In a diamond, they are joined up in a different way, to form the hardest substance known.

▼ Inside an atom

An atom is made up of different types of tiny particles. It looks like a small version of our Solar System. The central part – called the nucleus – is like our Sun. The electrons are arranged like the planets that fly around the Sun.

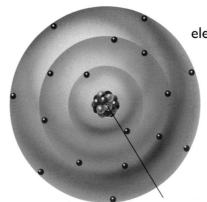

chlorine atom

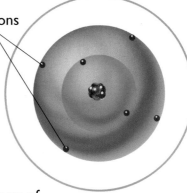

carbon atom

electrons

nucleus made up of protons and neutrons

◀ Water-works

One drop of water is made up of millions of molecules. Each of these molecules consists of one atom of oxygen and two atoms of hydrogen. Hydrogen and oxygen are themselves gases, but when they combine, they form water.

electromagnets speed the atoms on their way

tunnels

atoms speed round and round the tunnels, and are then directed by the magnets into the detector

particles collide here in the detector

◀ Atom-smasher

The only way to study atoms is to smash them open. To do this, scientists use a huge machine called a particle accelerator. The accelerator shoots atoms at each other very rapidly so that they collide.

Word box

collide
crash into each other

particle
tiny object that the eye cannot usually see

Babies

Human babies are very different from the babies of most other animals. This is because they are helpless and it takes several years before they are able to look after themselves.

◀ Early days

A newborn baby is very delicate. If it is born too early it may need extra care in hospital. This baby is in a heated box called an incubator. The pads measure vital things such as heartbeat.

◀ A close bond

Its mother's face is the first thing a baby recognizes. It soon learns to understand smiles and baby talk. The mother feels very close to her newborn baby. This closeness between parent and baby is called bonding, and is very important.

Word box

placenta
the part that supplies food to the baby inside the womb

womb
the part inside the mother's body where the baby develops

▼ How life starts

A baby starts to form when an 'egg' cell from the mother joins with a 'sperm' cell from the father. Thousands of tiny sperm cells may try to enter an egg cell to fertilize it (join with it), but only one will be successful.

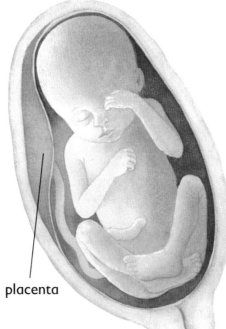

placenta

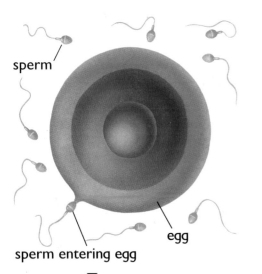

sperm

egg

sperm entering egg

▼ Making progress

As the baby develops, its progress can be checked with an ultrasound scanner. This uses sound waves to produce a picture of the baby in the womb. It is completely safe for the mother and her baby.

▲ Later stages

This shows a baby after six months in its mother's womb. It is very well developed, though still small. Over the next few weeks it will increase in size and will be born at around nine months. The developing baby feeds through a tubular cord. This joins its navel to the mother's placenta.

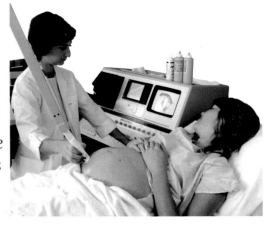

Birds

Birds are warm-blooded, but unlike other animals they are covered with feathers. Most birds can fly, and their bodies are built especially to make them very light.

◀ Grounded!

The ostrich is an unusual bird because it cannot fly. It is also heavy — strong enough to carry a man. These giants are the world's biggest birds and they live in Africa. They can run very fast to escape predators (hunters) such as lions.

▲ Giant of the skies

The huge condor of South America is the largest flying bird. It soars high over the Andes mountains, carried on warm air. As it goes, it looks out for dead or dying animals to eat, which it can see from far away.

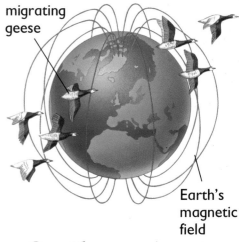

migrating geese

Earth's magnetic field

▲ On the move

Some birds travel a long way when they migrate. Even tiny swallows fly from Europe to Africa each autumn to avoid cold weather — 10,000 kilometres! Some birds find their way by sensing the direction of the Earth's natural magnetic field.

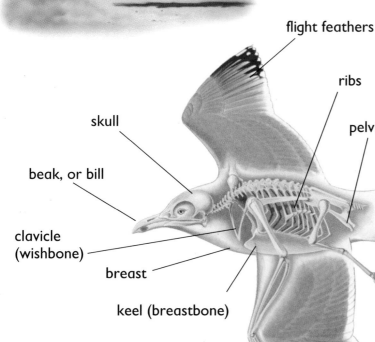

flight feathers

ribs

pelvis

tail feathers

skull

beak, or bill

clavicle (wishbone)

breast

keel (breastbone)

claw

▶ Made to fly

The body of a bird is specially adapted to help it fly. It has very large chest muscles to flap its wings. Many of its bones are hollow, filled with air, to save weight. Feathers cover almost all of the body. These increase the size of the wings, to help in flight. To eat, birds use a beak instead of teeth.

Wow!
The elephant bird, now extinct, was three times as big as an ostrich!

Blood

Blood is the life support system for our bodies. It carries the vital oxygen and goodness from food that we need for life and growth. It also helps to collect dangerous waste products from around the body.

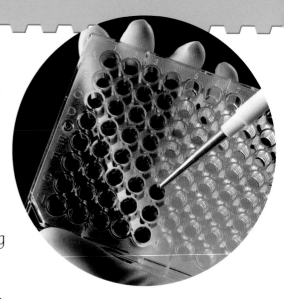

Word box

plasma
clear, yellowish liquid that makes up most of blood

transfusion
putting blood from a healthy person into someone who is sick or injured

▼ Blood cells

Blood contains several types of living cell, floating in a liquid called plasma. Red blood cells are tiny, flattish discs that take oxygen round the body. White cells fight infection. Tiny platelets help to stop bleeding.

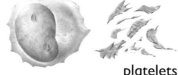

red blood cells

white blood cell

white blood cell

white blood cell

platelets

▲ Which group?

People who have lost a lot of blood through injury or disease may need a blood transfusion. It is vital that patients get blood from someone who has blood of the same group (type). To check this, small drops of blood from the person who is giving it are tested carefully beforehand.

▼ Under pressure

Blood is pumped under pressure round the body. Doctors often check this pressure, as it can cause problems if it is too high or low.

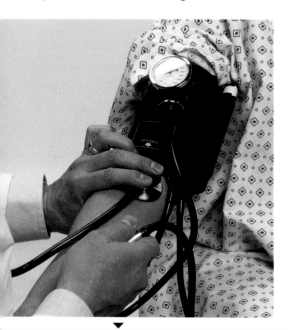

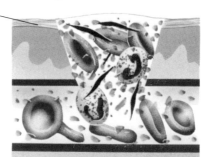

skin

sticky clot blocks the cut

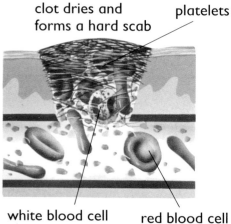

clot dries and forms a hard scab

platelets

white blood cell

red blood cell

▲ Stopping the flow

If you cut yourself, tiny structures called platelets release sticky substances. These block the cut with a mass of fibres to form a clot. White cells swarm into the cut to kill any germs, and repair begins. The mass of fibres and trapped red cells dry to form a scab. Underneath this, fresh skin develops.

Buildings

Find out more:
Materials in nature ▶ Materials now ▶

Since earliest times, we have needed buildings to protect us from the weather – and sometimes from enemies. The first buildings were made of straw, sticks and mud. Now we use much stronger materials such as concrete and steel.

▲ Fantasy castle

The eccentric King Ludwig of Bavaria built this extraordinary German castle in the 1700s. He designed it to look much older. The building borrows styles from various times of history, creating a fairytale fantasy castle.

Wow!

Many castles were built in India between 1500 and 1700. The gateways had iron spikes in the doors to stop war elephants breaking them down.

▲ Ancient ruins

The Colosseum is a huge amphitheatre (circular building) in Rome, Italy, built during the Roman Empire 2,000 years ago.

▶ Reaching for the sky

Modern buildings, such as skyscrapers, are built around a steel skeleton. Cranes are used to lift sections of the buildings into place.

Cells

Find out more:
Blood ◀ Genes ▶
Human body ▶

Your body is made from billions of tiny living units called cells. Different types of cell are grouped together to carry out particular jobs. Cells divide and multiply as we grow. They are replaced as they wear out.

lysosomes are like recycling centres, breaking up old and unwanted substances so their parts can be used again

cell membrane is the 'skin' around the cell and controls what comes in and goes out

mitochondria change food into energy to power the cell's processes

◀ Oxygen-carriers

This microscope photo of blood shows hundreds of red cells, which take oxygen around the body. The darker specks are white blood cells, which fight infection. They have been stained a dark colour to make them easier to see.

nucleus is the cell's control centre and contains the genetic material, DNA

ribosomes are ball-shaped factories that make useful substances or products

golgi layers wrap up the cell's products so they can be sent to where needed

Word box

plankton
tiny organisms that float in water

▲ Looking inside

All cells have the same basic form, although there are many different types. The nucleus controls how the cell works. It contains DNA, a material that contains a pattern for the development of the whole body.

axon

axon

signals jump gap

◀ Pass it on

Nerve cells carry messages round the body, in the form of electrical signals. These signals pass along the long, thin axon and then jump to the next nerve cell. Our brain, spinal cord and nerves are packed with millions of these cells.

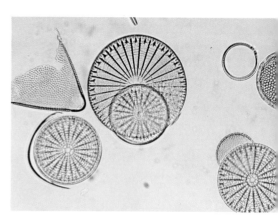

▲ Pond life

Have you seen green haze on a pond? This contains millions of microscopic plants, each made from a single cell. These are diatoms, and they live inside a hard, protective shell. Diatoms are also found at sea, floating in plankton.

Chemicals

Most of what is around us is made up of chemicals.
Plastic, soap, even water, are a mix of chemicals. Some chemicals are dangerous – chlorine for example. However, when chlorine is mixed with another chemical called sodium, salt is formed, which is harmless.

acidic substance, such as citric acid in lemons, turns red

neutral substance

alkaline substance turns purple

Fun and froth!
Make your own chemical reaction.
You will need: vinegar and washing soda
Add a few drops of vinegar to a spoonful of washing soda in a saucer. They will react with each other by frothing and giving off a gas called carbon dioxide.

▶ Chemical groups

Acids and bases are 'opposite' types of chemicals. They can be tested by using indicator paper, which changes colour when it touches different substances.

▶ Petroleum products

Petroleum, or crude oil, is a natural material that is used to make many different chemicals. Plastics, fuels, paint and soaps all come from crude oil. They are made in an oil refinery, where crude oil is heated in a huge tower. The oil is separated into different substances by boiling it at different temperatures.

oil refinery tower

crude oil turns to gas and rises up tower

crude oil is heated in a furnace

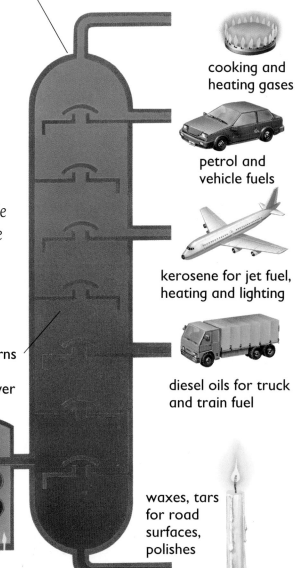

cooking and heating gases

petrol and vehicle fuels

kerosene for jet fuel, heating and lighting

diesel oils for truck and train fuel

waxes, tars for road surfaces, polishes

▼ Chemical colours

Fireworks use chemicals to make wonderful displays. Inside them are tiny metal particles, or chemicals that contain metal. They also contain substances that produce oxygen. When these burn together, each metal produces a different coloured flame – and exciting sparks!

Climate

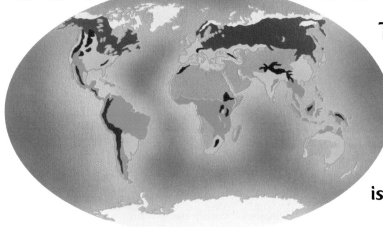

The Earth moving around the Sun causes certain weather patterns that are repeated regularly. These patterns are called climate. The climate is always hot in Africa, for example, and cold in the far North. In Europe, the climate is temperate – neither too hot nor too cold.

- ░ Polar (cold)
- ■ Continental temperate (mild)
- ■ Mountain (cold at height)
- ▒ Moist temperate (mild and wet)
- ▒ Tropical (warm all year)
- ▒ Desert (dry and hot)

Wow!
Siberia, in eastern Russia, has the biggest difference between summer and winter. Temperatures vary from 15° Celsius in July to -51° Celsius in January!

▲ Climate zones

The surface of the Earth has zones (areas) where the climate is usually similar. For instance, the climate in North America and northern Europe is very similar. So is the climate at the North and South Poles.

◀ Deep drifts

Heavy snowfalls and high winds can be very dangerous. Snow that is blown by the wind can pile up into large mounds called drifts. These may bring traffic to a halt and cause accidents. Drifts may also prevent animals from eating grass buried beneath the snow.

▼ Desert regions

Deserts form in areas where there is very little rainfall. Some are sandy, others are mostly rock and stones. There are also some cold deserts, such as the Gobi Desert in China during winter.

Climate change

Find out more:
Air ◄ Conservation ► Energy sources ►
Pollution ► Weather ►

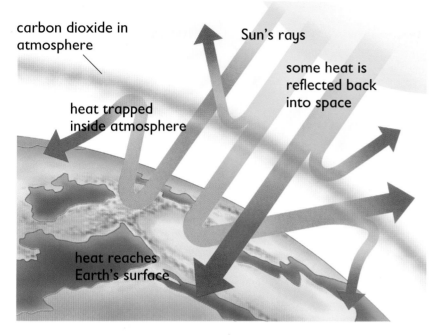

carbon dioxide in atmosphere

Sun's rays

some heat is reflected back into space

heat trapped inside atmosphere

heat reaches Earth's surface

Climates can change. This may be caused by a warm ocean current changing position. Humans also cause change, by doing things such as cutting down tropical forests. This may reduce rainfall over a wide area, turning it into desert.

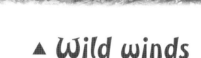

▲ Getting warmer

When we burn fuels such as coal, oil and wood, a gas called carbon dioxide is released into the air. Large amounts of this gas trap the Sun's energy — the 'greenhouse effect'. This raises the air temperature, just as glass on a greenhouse traps heat inside. This is known as 'global warming'.

▼ Rising waters

As the climate changes with global warming, polar ice is melting. This makes the sea level rise. Some low coral islands in the Pacific Ocean have already vanished, and others may follow.

Word box

coral
hard, stony material produced by tiny animals in tropical seas

hurricane
giant storm with high winds

▲ Wild winds

Changes in climate may increase the number of hurricanes that sweep in from the sea. These can cause enormous damage, due to the great power of the wind and the floods that often follow.

▶ Ice Ages ago

The 'Ice Age' was made up of several cold and warm periods, each lasting many thousands of years. During the last Ice Age, around fifteen thousand years ago, ice sheets covered the land. Early humans were well adapted to the cold conditions.

Colour

Try this!

Have fun mixing lots of colours with your paints. Blue, yellow and red are the primary paint colours (these are different from the primary light colours – see 'Mixing light'). See how many different colours you can come up with. You'll be amazed!

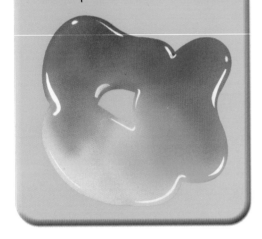

When we look at an object, we do not actually *see* its colour. Instead, we see the light that the object reflects, or bounces off. White light (a mix of all colours) falls on the object, but most of its colours are soaked up or absorbed. The colours that are reflected reach our eyes and give the object its colour. So, we see a leaf as green because it absorbs all other coloured light except green.

◀ Mixing light

Red, green and blue are the 'primary' colours of light. They can be mixed together to produce any other colour. When two primaries are mixed, they make a 'secondary' colour. If equal amounts of all primary light colours are mixed together, they make white light.

Red
Yellow Magenta
White
Green Cyan Blue

▼ Natural colour

Flowers are brightly coloured to attract insects such as bees, which help to pollinate them (make them reproduce). Bees' eyes can see colours and patterns that are invisible to us.

▶ The spectrum

Here, ordinary white light is being passed through a triangular piece of glass called a prism. This splits the light into its different colours. The whole range of bands of colour is called a spectrum. You can sometimes see this effect around the edge of a thick mirror, or when sunlight shines through a vase of water.

◀ On the page

Colour pictures in magazines and books and on TV screens are actually made up of thousands of tiny dots of colour. Our eyes naturally mix these colours together.

Our whole life is based on communication. We communicate when we speak or wave to someone, and when we send a letter. Modern technology allows us to communicate at very high speeds right across the world – by telephone, radio, television or the Internet.

▲ Internet phone

This mobile phone lets you make voice calls, browse the Internet and send text messages and emails. Some allow you to listen to the radio or even watch TV.

▶ Let's communicate!

As well as words, we use a lot of 'body language' to communicate with people – often to say hello or goodbye. Hand gestures, facial expressions, body positions and eye contact are all ways of communicating with others.

Wow!
One of the longest phone calls ever recorded lasted for 550 hours – nearly a whole month!

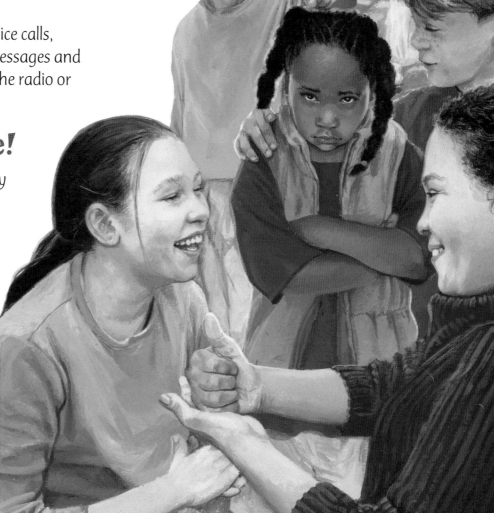

Computers

Computers are complicated machines that can process huge amounts of information in a very short time. They are not intelligent themselves, but they help us to do clever things that we would not be able to do on our own. For example, computers can now beat humans at chess.

Wow!

Special computers are used to calculate the weather forecast. Some can work out a six-day global forecast in just 15 minutes!

▲ Early computers

One of the first proper computers was called *Colossus*. It was built in 1943 to decode (work out) complex messages used by Germany during World War II. It stayed a great secret for another 40 years.

Word box

circuit
a loop of electricity

microchip
tiny slice of a substance called silicon, containing millions of electronic parts

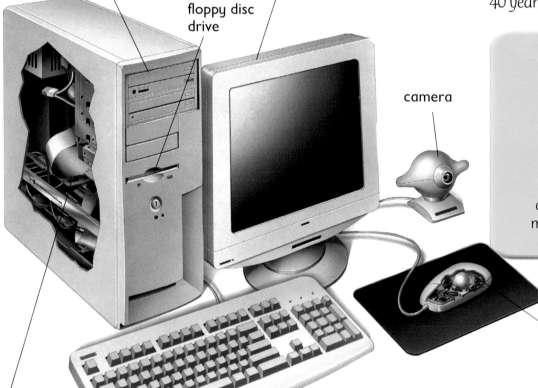

CD-ROM drive reads information from a compact disc

floppy disc drive

monitor (screen) displays information from the computer

camera

mouse

the microprocessor is the computer's main microchip and controls the computer

keyboard

▲ What goes where?

Computers have a keyboard, a screen, a mouse and a main box that contains electronic circuits that control computer processes. Some of the latest computers have a flat screen. The mouse is a hand-held device that allows you to control the computer quickly and conveniently.

Conservation

Many animals and plants are in danger of dying out, or becoming extinct. Their habitat may have been destroyed by pollution or deforestation, while some animals may have been hunted for their fur or meat. Conservation is important for protecting all of these living things.

▲ National parks

To try and conserve wild parts of the world, large areas have been set aside as national parks. Here, building, tourism and other activities are strongly controlled.

▲ Saving the panda

China is trying to preserve its giant pandas by breeding them in captivity. Farming is destroying the places where the pandas live. They are also hunted for their skins.

◀ Empty seas

For thousands of years, the sea has provided fish for us to eat. But now modern fishing boats are able to catch more fish than can be replaced. Fish that were once very common, such as cod, are in danger of being wiped out.

◀ The last orchid

Human actions have made some wild plants so rare that they need to be protected. The rare lady's slipper orchids grows only in one place — in Yorkshire, England. Its location is kept secret in order to protect it.

Word box

deforestation
cutting down large areas of forest

habitat
home

▲ Saving our trees

All over the world, forests are being felled (cut down) for timber, and to provide farming land. Some forests are lost forever, but now many are specially replanted so that they can continue to supply us with timber.

Crystals

Most crystals are formed from minerals – natural substances found in the Earth's crust. They come in different shapes, but all have straight edges and flat surfaces. Some crystals, such as salt, are simple cubes. But other substances produce crystals with more complex shapes.

◀ Sugary crystals

The sugar you use at home is actually tiny crystals. Water is slowly made to evaporate (disappear into the air) from sugar syrup, so that solid sugar is left lumpy as crystals.

▲ Inside snow

Snow is made up of millions of tiny ice crystals. These form inside cold clouds, where they collide and stick together to produce snowflakes. Some snowflakes have star shapes with six sides like this, others look like long needles of ice.

▲ Spiky shapes

Amethyst crystals are formed from a mineral called quartz. With its many different surfaces and angles, this is a good example of crystals with a complex shape.

◀ Liquid crystal

The LCD (liquid crystal display) screen of this hand-held television is made up of 'liquid' crystals. These are crystals that have been heated up so they become cloudy. Thousands of liquid crystals build up to make the image you see on the screen.

Try this!

Put hot tap water (careful!) in a jam jar. Now pour in salt, stirring until it has all dissolved. Let the water cool. Tiny salt crystals will slowly form on the bottom of the jar. Use a spoon to remove most of the crystals, leaving just one or two of the largest. Put the jar somewhere warm and check it every week. As the water evaporates, the salt crystals will grow in size.

Dinosaurs

Dinosaurs were the biggest land animals that ever lived. They were reptiles that first appeared 240 million years ago. These creatures were the Earth's most successful life-form, until they died out 64 million years ago.

▲ Why did they die?

No one is certain why the dinosaurs became extinct (died out). There were many volcanic eruptions at this time, and some scientists think that dust and fumes could have killed them. Others believe the Earth was struck by a huge meteorite from space, which changed the climate so they could not survive.

▲ Looking after baby

Some dinosaurs looked after their young. Eggs were laid in mud nests in huge colonies (groups). The babies were guarded by their parents until they were large enough to look after themselves. Crocodiles, which are also reptiles, still care for their babies in this way.

Tyrannosaurus rex

Wow!

The name dinosaur means 'terrible lizard'. But dinosaurs weren't actually lizards, and not all dinosaurs were terrible either!

Triceratops

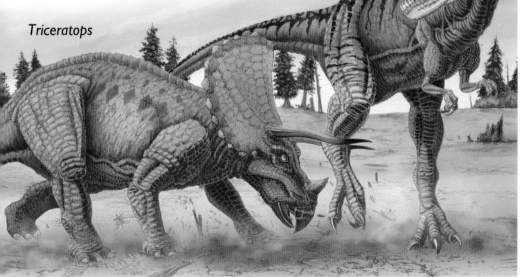

◀ Deadly enemies

Many plant-eating dinosaurs had to protect themselves against deadly attackers, such as the fierce *Tyrannosaurus rex*. *Triceratops* had large horns and spikes, and hard lumps of bone, which acted as a kind of armour.

Earth

Word box

atmosphere
layers of air surrounding the Earth

crust
outer layer of cold, hard rock covering the Earth

mantle
layer of soft rock, just below the Earth's crust

Our Earth is the third planet out from the Sun, positioned between Mars and Venus. Earth is different from all of our neighbouring planets because we have oceans and a breathable atmosphere. This is why life has developed here.

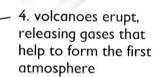

1. cloud starts to spin

4. volcanoes erupt, releasing gases that help to form the first atmosphere

3. the Earth begins to cool and a hard shell forms

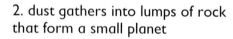

2. dust gathers into lumps of rock that form a small planet

▲ The Earth is born

The Earth is thought to have formed about 4,600 million years ago. It may have started as a huge cloud of swirling dust and gases.

▶ Layer upon layer

The Earth consists of layers. At the centre is a mass of very hot iron and nickel, called the core. The solid layer of rock that covers the Earth is called the crust. Just below the crust is the mantle, made of hot, soft rock. These layers are pulled together by a force called gravity.

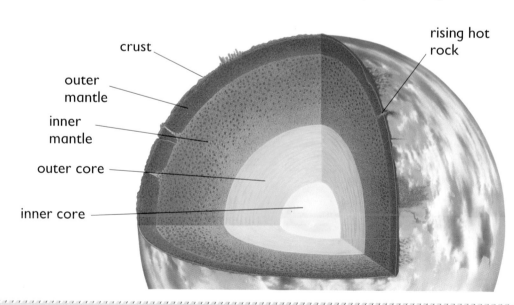

crust
outer mantle
inner mantle
outer core
inner core
rising hot rock

Earth features

Over millions of years, features such as mountains, rivers and deserts have appeared on the Earth's surface. Mountains, for example, have been formed by movements of the Earth's crust. Many features have then been shaped by water and weather.

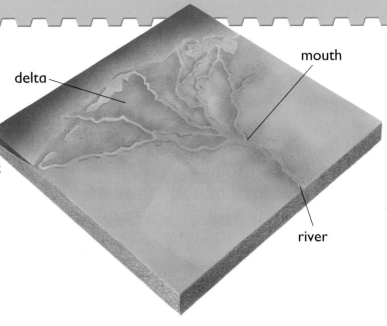

delta

mouth

river

▲ The river's end

A delta is an area of flat land at the mouth of a river, where it flows into the sea. The land is formed as material, called sediment, builds up quicker than it can be washed away by the sea's currents. The river splits into narrower channels as it crosses the delta and travels to the sea.

arch

stack

bay

▲ Shaping the shore

The seashore is always changing. The constant motion of the waves beats against the coastline. This wears away cliffs and beaches, leaving features such as arches, stacks and bays.

Wow!
The Dead Sea, in the Middle East, contains so much salt that you can float on it like a lilo!

▼ Shifting plates

Some mountains are formed by volcanoes. Most are produced by huge 'plates' of crust that make up the continents. When they shift, these plates may collide or overlap so that rocks rise up into ridges. This happens over millions of years.

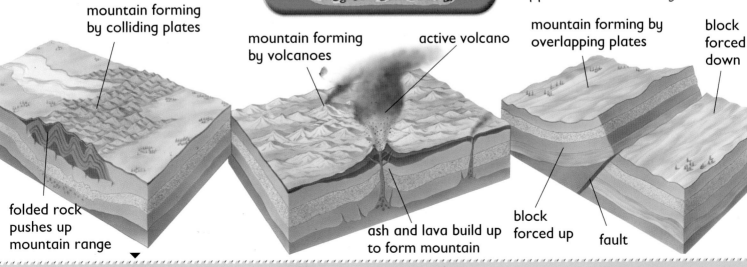

mountain forming by colliding plates

mountain forming by volcanoes

active volcano

mountain forming by overlapping plates

block forced down

folded rock pushes up mountain range

ash and lava build up to form mountain

block forced up

fault

Electricity

Find out more:
Atoms and molecules ◄ Electricity in action ►
Energy ► Energy sources ► Machines ►

Many machines are powered by electricity, because it is clean and cheap. Electricity is produced in power stations, sometimes by burning coal, oil or gas, and sometimes by nuclear power or by the use of water to turn huge turbines. It is sent along a network of cables supported by metal towers called pylons.

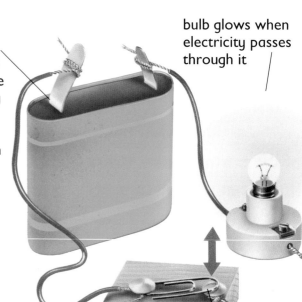

a battery contains chemicals that make electricity when the switch is turned on

bulb glows when electricity passes through it

a switch turns electricity off and on by breaking the circuit and joining it again

► Plus to minus

In a simple electric circuit, current flows from the positive (+) pole of a battery to the negative (-) pole.
If the current flows through a light bulb, the 'resistance' of the thin metal filament (thread) inside the bulb produces heat and light.

▲ Solar panels

The light or heat energy from the Sun can be turned directly into electricity by devices called solar panels. A panel does not produce much power, so many are usually joined into banks of panels. They need strong sunlight to work well, and are mostly used in hot and sunny climates.

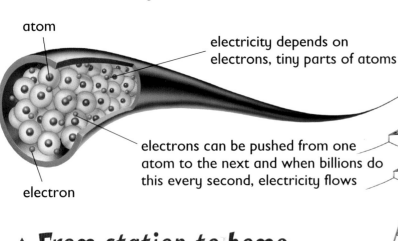

atom

electron

electricity depends on electrons, tiny parts of atoms

electrons can be pushed from one atom to the next and when billions do this every second, electricity flows

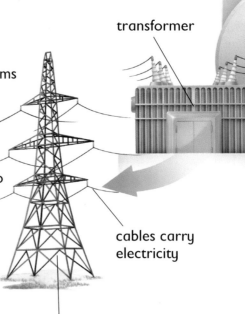

power station

transformer

cables carry electricity

pylon holds cables safe, far above the ground

the battery or generator at a power station gives the 'push' that starts the electrons on their journey

▲ From station to home

From the generator, electricity passes to 'transformers', which produce high voltages (how the strength of electricity is measured). This electricity is then carried by cables into homes and factories.

Electricity in action

Electricity is constantly at work around you.
You switch lights on and off or watch the television. Cars need electricity to start their engines, and most trains are powered by electricity. Electricity is also produced by natural things, such as lightning, and is even present inside our own bodies.

▼ Electric fun

Electricity can be used for decoration and for fun. Fairgrounds rely on plenty of coloured lights and rides powered by electricity.

◄ Hair-raiser

Static electricity is the same as flowing electricity except that it does not move. It can make a push or pull effect like a magnet – which can be very hair-raising!

► Charge!

A mobile phone's battery is rechargeable. This means that when the battery runs down, the chemicals inside can be recharged by sending electricity through them.

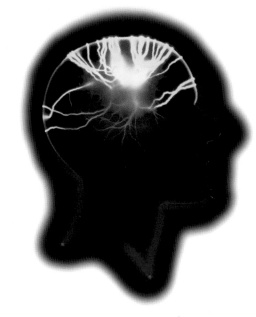

▲ Human electricity

The human body produces tiny electrical signals by chemical reactions in the nerve cells. These are insulated (covered) like an electric cable, to prevent the signals from leaking away.

Make a circuit

You will need: a lightbulb, some wire, a 3-volt battery, a plastic ruler, a metal spoon, some dry card

Ask an adult to help. Join the lightbulb to the battery with pieces of wire, as shown below. Electricity flows round the circuit and lights the bulb. Make a gap in the circuit and put various objects there instead, such as the ruler. See if they allow electricity to flow again.

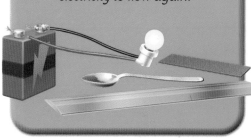

Energy

Everything around us needs energy to work. Heat, light, movement and sound are all forms of energy. Plants need energy from the Sun to survive. We need energy to lead our daily lives. Energy can be changed from one form into another, such as burning oil or coal to create heat.

Word box

chlorophyll
green substance inside the leaves of a plant. It uses the Sun's energy to help make sugar to feed the plant

▲ Feel the heat

Heat is just one form of energy. It can be stored in many ways. When you cup your hands round a hot drink in cold weather, you are using some of the heat energy in the drink to warm your own hands.

► From Sun to sugar

Plants use energy from the Sun, in the form of light. They use a green substance called chlorophyll to change the light energy into sugars, which they can store. The energy is still held in the sugar and is released when the plant needs it.

▲ Our world

Electricity is a very important form of energy for our modern world. We need huge amounts of electricity for lighting, heat, transport and lots of other things that we do. We have many ways of creating this energy, using coal, oil, nuclear power and water power.

► In the air

Sound is a type of energy that causes vibrations in the air. When these reach your ears, the energy moves tiny bones inside the ear. This changes the sound energy into movement, then into electrical signals. The signals go to your brain to tell you what you are hearing.

▼ Body-power

We need energy to power muscles and keep our bodies working. We get this from food, which is turned into substances that can be stored. The energy is then released when it is needed.

Energy sources

All the energy we use comes from the Sun. Plants use the Sun's energy to grow. Long ago, plants died and then over millions of years turned into coal. When we burn coal, energy is released. Also, the Sun lets us grow food, which our bodies turn into movement energy.

▲ Energy on a plate

Food gives us energy to power our bodies. Foods such as sugar give you almost immediate energy. Fat and protein, mostly obtained from meat, produce energy needed over longer periods.

Word box

generator
a machine that changes movement energy into electricity

▼ On the wind

There are strong winds along many coasts, and in mountainous places. The energy from this wind can be turned into electricity. This is done at huge wind 'farms' where giant windmills drive electric generators.

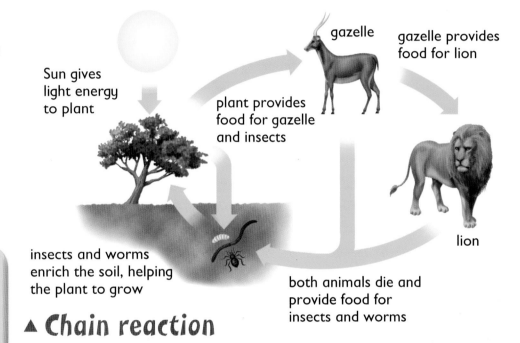

Sun gives light energy to plant

plant provides food for gazelle and insects

gazelle

gazelle provides food for lion

lion

both animals die and provide food for insects and worms

insects and worms enrich the soil, helping the plant to grow

▲ Chain reaction

This picture shows a typical 'food chain' – how all our energy comes from the Sun. The plants make their food from sunlight and soil, and are then eaten by plant-eaters, such as gazelles. These in turn are eaten by meat-eaters, such as lions. When any animal dies, insects break down the body and enrich the soil, allowing more plants to grow. So the cycle continues.

► Underground power

Energy from the Sun is used and stored by plants. Millions of years ago, plants died and were gradually buried beneath the ground. They decayed (wasted away) under great pressure from the layers of rock above them. This turned them slowly into coal.

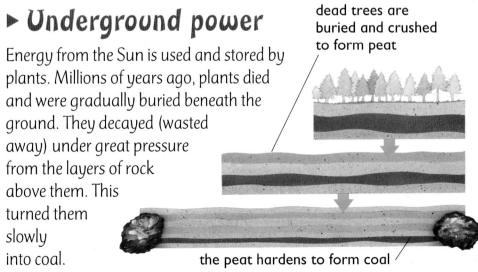

dead trees are buried and crushed to form peat

the peat hardens to form coal

Engines

The invention of engines allowed us to control and change the world around us. Engines let us travel. They let us transport very heavy materials around the world. Engines also power the machinery we need to mine coal and important minerals.

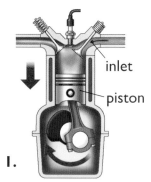

1.

▲ piston moves down to suck in fuel and air

inlet
piston

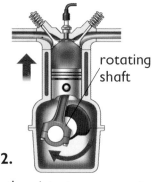

2.

▲ the piston moves up to squeeze the fuel and air

rotating shaft

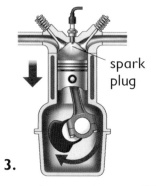

3.

▲ spark sets mixture alight pushing piston down

spark plug

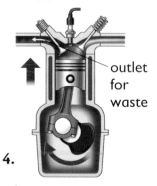

4.

▲ the piston moves up to push out waste gases

outlet for waste

◄ How petrol engines work

Air and fuel is pushed into a cylinder. Tiny explosions caused by 'spark plugs' keep the piston moving up and down. This makes the shaft rotate, which connects to gears so that the wheels go round. Most cars have petrol engines.

Word box

cylinder
tube in which fuel is burned

diesel
an engine fuelled by diesel oil instead of petrol, that has no spark plugs

smokestack
boiler
firebox

▲ The power of steam

Steam engines helped to develop our modern civilization. Early locomotives were steam-driven, powered by coal or wood. They have mostly been replaced by diesel or electric trains. However, steam trains are still used in some poorer countries.

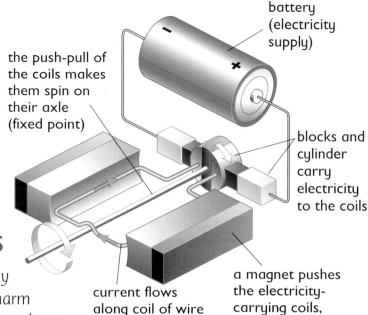

battery (electricity supply)

the push-pull of the coils makes them spin on their axle (fixed point)

blocks and cylinder carry electricity to the coils

current flows along coil of wire

a magnet pushes the electricity-carrying coils, which have their own magnetism

► Electric motors

Some of the fumes given out by petrol and diesel engines can harm the environment. For this reason, electric motors are now becoming more common in vehicles. They are powered by batteries and are cleaner, quieter and more reliable.

Fish

Find out more:
Animal kingdom ◄ Animal life ◄
Water ► Water and life ►

Fish are a group of animals that are adapted to live in water. They are usually covered in scales, which protect their body. Fish breathe oxygen dissolved in the water, as it passes over parts called gills.

▼ Inside a fish

Most of the parts of a fish are squeezed into the front of the body. The rear of the body is made up of powerful swimming muscles. A fish's swim bladder is an important part that helps it to float easily at any depth.

▲ Fierce hunters

Sharks are the sea's biggest, fiercest predatory fish. This ancient family are very primitive. Their bodies are supported by gristly cartilage, not bone. Sharks eat fish, seals and other sea life. Attacking people is very rare.

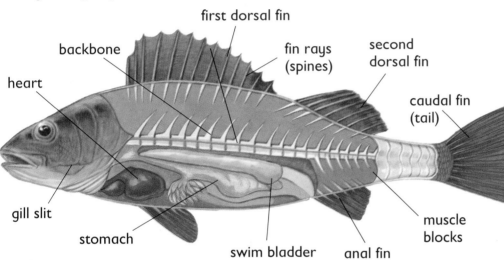

- first dorsal fin
- backbone
- fin rays (spines)
- second dorsal fin
- heart
- caudal fin (tail)
- gill slit
- muscle blocks
- stomach
- swim bladder
- anal fin

Word scramble

Unscramble these words to find the names of four different fish:

a. NUTA
b. SNOMAL
c. KRHAS
d. DOC

answers
a. tuna b. salmon c. shark d. cod

Word box

predator
an animal that hunts and eats other animals

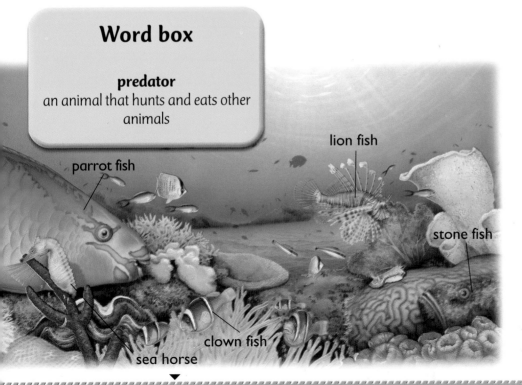

- parrot fish
- lion fish
- stone fish
- clown fish
- sea horse

◄ Rainbow fish

Thousands of different types of fish live in the shallow and sunny coral waters. Most of these fish have colourful spots or stripes. This makes it hard for a hunter to spot them swimming through the coral.

Food gives us energy to move and keep warm.
Without it, we could not survive. People used to gather or
farm their own food. Today, big businesses and complex
scientific processes are needed to provide enough food for
lots of people and to send it long distances.

Look inside food

Look at the labels on some food
packages. They tell you how much
carbohydrate, protein, fats and
sugar the foods contain. Some also
tell you how many vitamins and
minerals there are in the food.

◄ Totally tropical!

Tropical fruits grow
mainly in the
tropics where it is
warm, as they
cannot survive frost. The
best known are bananas,
pineapples and melons. Large
quantities of these are exported
(shipped to other countries). Other
tropical fruits include guavas,
breadfruit, mangoes and papayas.

◄ Italian favourite

Pizza was invented by
the Italians. The word
'pizza' is Italian for pie. It
is thought to have first
been made by a baker at the
royal court in Naples, southern
Italy, during the 1700s. Pizza is now
a favourite food around the world.

milk contains calcium,
a mineral that gives you
strong bones

carbohydrates are found
in bread, pasta, potatoes
and rice – they give
you energy

fresh fruits
and
vegetables
contain lots of
vitamins and
minerals.
They help you
fight disease,
keeping you
fit and healthy

► What's in food?

Food contains special substances
called nutrients. There are six
main kinds of nutrients –
carbohydrates, fats, proteins,
fibre, vitamins and minerals. You
need the right amounts of all
these nutrients to stay healthy.

proteins in cheese, meat,
eggs, nuts and fish help you
grow and keep your body
strong

fats from foods such as butter, oil
and cheese give you energy and
healthy nerves

fibre is important for helping the
digestive system to work properly.
Fruit and vegetables are fibre-rich

Forces

Forces are the natural properties of the world around us. Engines produce forces that make machines work. Without the force of gravity, we would fly off the world's surface, as the Earth spins. Friction is a force that stops us from slipping over. Inertia stops us from being pushed over by a gust of wind.

◄ Wind force

Wind provides the force that pushes a sailing boat along. As the wind flows over the sail, it creates high pressure on the inner curved surface. This pushes against the lower pressure on the other outer side of the sail. The difference in pressure makes a force that moves the boat.

Slip and slide!

Place a stone on a sheet of wood, then tilt the wood until the stone begins to slide. Now spread washing-up liquid on the wood and try again. See how the stone slides much more easily. Like oil, the washing-up liquid is a lubricant, reducing friction.

▲ Pulling power

Gravity pulls a heavy object down. However, the object can be lifted by using a stronger force, pulling on a rope passing over a pulley.

◄ Under pressure

The force of gravity on our bodies produces pressure where we stand on the ground. This is why footprints show up on snow or mud.

▼ Keep moving!

There is a natural law (rule) which says that, once something is set in motion, it will carry on in the same direction and at the same speed until some other forces act on it. Air resistance or friction will slow this ball down. Gravity will pull it towards the ground.

the ball is kicked

path of the ball without gravity or air resistance

air resistance

path of ball when gravity and air resistance are at work

air resistance

gravity pushes down on the ball

gravity pushes down on the ball

Fossils

Long, long ago, the remains of some dead animals and plants became fossils – that is, turned into stone. This happened because they were covered with mud. Over time, the mud turned into rock, along with the remains inside. Usually, just hard parts like bones or shells remain, turned to stone. But we can still see how the animal looked.

▲ Sea fossils

The snail-shaped shells of ammonites are very common fossils. They lived in the seas many millions of years ago, but became extinct (died out) quite suddenly. They were related to the modern octopus, and some produced shells as big as one metre across.

Wow!

Teeth from giant sharks have been found that are as big as an adult's hand!

▲ Light and strong

This is the preserved skull of the dinosaur *T. rex*. From this skull, we can see that it had huge, powerful jaws and enormous teeth. These let it kill and feed on other dinosaurs.

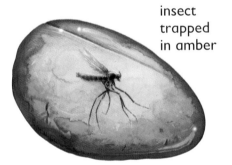

insect trapped in amber

▲ Studying the past

The study of fossils is called palaeontology. When fossils are found, palaeontologists help to uncover them carefully and to preserve them. Fossils are very heavy and brittle, so they are wrapped in plaster to prevent any damage. People work with great care to expose (uncover) the fossils and strengthen them so they can be shown in museums.

▲ Trapped in time

The bark of trees like pines sometimes produces a sticky, liquid resin. Insects get stuck in this resin. Over millions of years, ancient tree resin became fossilized. Golden amber is fossilized resin. Many pieces contain perfectly preserved insects.

Genes

Find out more:
Cells ◄ Human body ►

Word box

inherit
you inherit something passed on from your parents in their genes, such as your eye or hair colour

Genes are the tiny sets of instructions inside our cells that control how we develop and how we look. These have been passed on from our parents' cells. So, you might get your eye colour from your father and your hair colour from your mother. All living things have genes that control the way they grow and look.

DNA has a spiral shape like a twisted rope ladder

each 'rung' contains two special chemicals

▲ Pass it on!

Several generations (ages) of a family share similar genes. New genes may come into a family when its members marry. But because each of us has so many genes, some of the original ones stay in a family for centuries.

father has both blue and brown eye genes

mother has both blue and brown eye genes

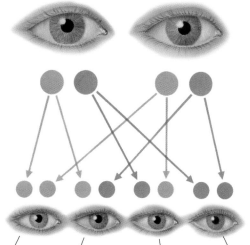

two brown eye genes will give brown eyes

one brown gene and one blue will give brown eyes

one blue gene and one brown will give brown eyes

two blue eye genes will give blue eyes

the four possible combinations

◄ Which gene?

You inherit genes from both parents. The way these genes were mixed when you were conceived controls how you look. In this example, both parents had genes for blue and brown eyes. Brown eye genes are stronger ('dominant') than those for blue eyes.

▲ Thread of life

Coiled up inside each cell of your body are molecules called DNA. Genes are small areas along threads of DNA. Each gene controls some tiny part of the way the cell and your body works. They store information about your body like the hard disk in a computer. The whole body needs about 40,000 genes and all of these are in each cell.

Gravity

Find out more:
Energy ◄ Forces ◄

Gravity is a natural force that tries to press us down towards the centre of the Earth. It is gravity that stops you from jumping very high. Astronauts need immense rockets to break away from the Earth's gravity when they travel into space.

◄ Floating in space

The further away an object is from the centre of the Earth, the less the pull of gravity on it. In space, astronauts are so far from the Earth's centre that gravity has little effect on them. They become weightless, so that when they move around, they appear to be floating.

▲ Weightless in water

The only easy way for you to feel weightless is floating or swimming. The water supports your weight so you do not feel gravity pulling you down.

Wow!

When astronauts go to sleep in space, they have to strap themselves to their beds so that they don't float around!

▼ Using friction

On a rollercoaster ride, the force of gravity moves the car. Gravity pulls the car faster downhill but also slows the car down as it climbs the uphill parts of the ride. Air friction slows the car, too, until it coasts gently to a halt once all of its stored energy has been used.

Health

Good health is the result of eating the right foods, taking exercise and getting enough rest. These all help to keep your body working properly. Looking after your health in this way makes it less likely that you will become ill.

◄ Sleeping soundly

We know that too little sleep can affect our health. Young babies sleep for most of the time. Many elderly people need less sleep than when they were younger because they are less active.

▲ Long life

Some of the oldest people in the world live in countries like Japan. There, the diet is very different from a Western one. In areas where people are long-lived, they usually eat simple diets, such as raw fish. This is full of vitamins and protein, but low in fat.

▼ Keeping fit

Exercise such as running, cycling or walking is vital for developing strong muscles, and keeping your heart healthy. It is just as important for adults, to prevent diseases as the body gets older.

▼ Health checks

Even when you feel perfectly healthy, you should have regular check-ups at the doctor's. Many health problems can be spotted early on and treated before they get worse. Checks on the teeth and eyes are very important.

▲ Healthy food

Many of us eat too much ready-prepared, processed food. Eating fresh food is very important. For example, we should all eat plenty of fresh fruit and vegetables. However, if we store them for too long or over-cook them, we destroy their goodness.

Heat

Heat is an important form of energy. It is produced in our own bodies as we break down and use the food we eat. We can release stored heat energy by burning fuels such as wood or coal. Heat can move from one substance to another in three different ways: by convection, by radiation and by conduction.

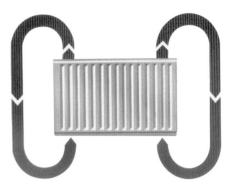

▲ Heat: convection

Above a radiator, warmed air gets lighter and rises. Cold air moves in to replace it, and is heated up. This is called 'convection'.

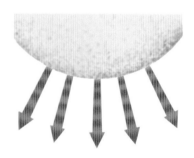

▲ Heat: radiation

Radiation is rays of energy. The Sun's rays travel through space and reach us as heat and light energy.

▲ Releasing energy

When we burn wood or coal on a fire, we start a chemical reaction that releases energy stored in the fuel. Flames are the area where substances in the fuel combine with oxygen in the air to release energy as heat and light.

Heat-carriers

Ask an adult to help. Take a metal spoon, a wooden ruler and a plastic spatula. Fix a frozen pea to one end of each with butter. Put the other ends in a jug of hot water. Heat is conducted from the water up each object, melting the butter. One of the objects is the best conductor – which one is it?

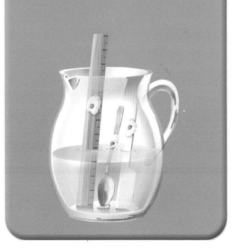

Word box

conductor
a substance that heat or electricity passes through easily

insulator
a substance that does not conduct heat or electricity well

▲ Heat: conduction

Conduction is the way heat spreads through a solid or liquid object. Metal is a faster conductor than glass.

Heat and temperature

While heat is a form of energy, temperature is a measure of heat. Temperature tells us how hot or cold something is, or how much heat it contains. It is measured in degrees Celsius (°C) or Fahrenheit (°F) or the absolute temperature scale, measured in kelvins (K).

solar panel

pipes of hot water

15,000,000°C	Centre of Sun
30,000°C	Inside lightning bolt
5,000°C	Centre of Earth
1,000°C	Lava from volcano
200 °C	Oil in frying pan
100°C	Boiling water
37°C	Body temperature
0°C	Water freezes
−78.5°C	Solid carbon dioxide ('dry ice')
Absolute zero −273.16°C	

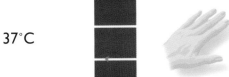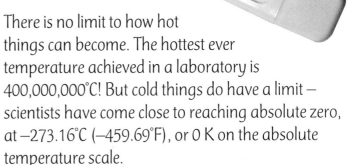

▲ Using the Sun

In some countries, houses are centrally heated using solar (sun) energy. A solar panel filled with liquid is placed on the roof of the house. The Sun's warmth heats up the liquid, which passes into the house to heat up radiators and hot water.

▼ How warm are you?

A thermometer is used for measuring heat. Digital thermometers contain an electronic part that is sensitive to heat. Your normal body temperature is about 37 degrees Celsius (°C), or 98.6 degrees Fahrenheit (°F).

◄ Heat extremes

There is no limit to how hot things can become. The hottest ever temperature achieved in a laboratory is 400,000,000°C! But cold things do have a limit – scientists have come close to reaching absolute zero, at −273.16°C (−459.69°F), or 0 K on the absolute temperature scale.

Human body

Find out more:
Blood ◄ Cells ◄ Food ◄ Health ◄ Human senses ►

Your body is one of the most complicated living things. It runs itself almost automatically, provided you eat and drink when necessary. It contains several systems which look after different functions, such as breathing, digestion and movement. The most complicated of these is the nervous system, including the brain.

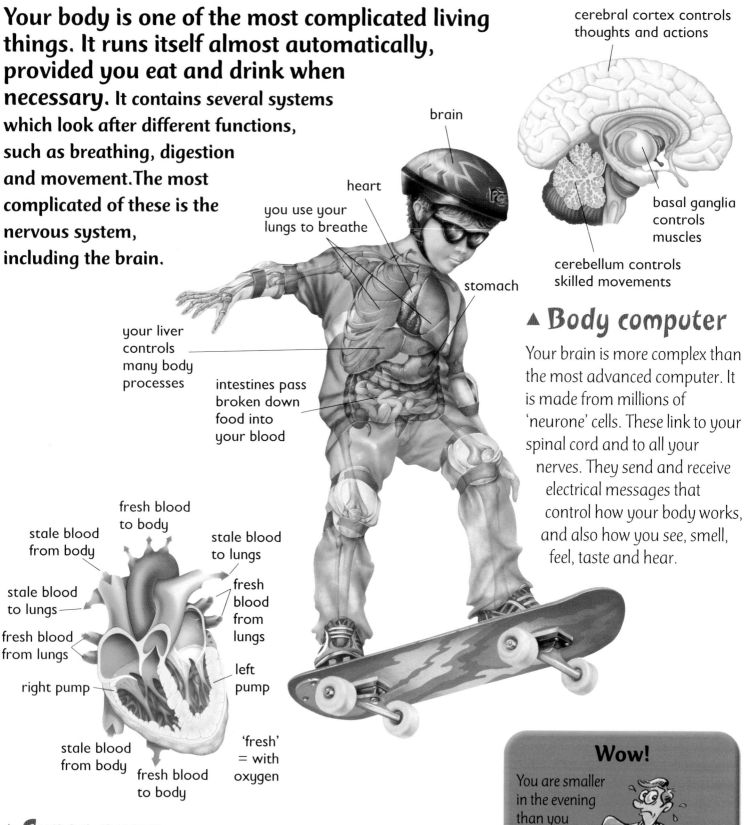

brain

heart

you use your lungs to breathe

stomach

your liver controls many body processes

intestines pass broken down food into your blood

cerebral cortex controls thoughts and actions

basal ganglia controls muscles

cerebellum controls skilled movements

▲ Body computer

Your brain is more complex than the most advanced computer. It is made from millions of 'neurone' cells. These link to your spinal cord and to all your nerves. They send and receive electrical messages that control how your body works, and also how you see, smell, feel, taste and hear.

fresh blood to body

stale blood from body

stale blood to lungs

stale blood to lungs

fresh blood from lungs

fresh blood from lungs

left pump

right pump

stale blood from body

'fresh' = with oxygen

fresh blood to body

Wow!
You are smaller in the evening than you are in the morning!

▲ Super-pump

Your heart is a pair of pumps made mostly from muscle. It makes sure blood collects oxygen from the lungs and travels round the body. 'Valves' keep the flow in the right direction.

Human senses

**Our senses make us aware of the outside world.
We use our sense organs to see, hear, touch, taste and smell
our surroundings. As well as these five senses, we also have
a sixth sense called balance. This enables us to stand and
move about on two legs.**

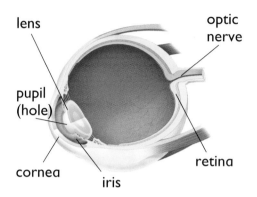

lens
optic nerve
pupil (hole)
cornea
iris
retina

▲ How we see

Light enters the eye through a clear layer at the front. It passes through a lens that focuses light on the retina, at the back. This causes 'receptors' to send nerve signals to the brain. The brain 'sees' these as pictures.

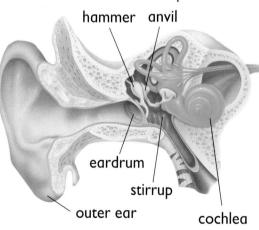

hammer   anvil
eardrum
stirrup
outer ear
cochlea

▲ Pass it along

Sound waves vibrate the ear drum and pass on to tiny bony levers inside the skull. Hairs inside the coiled cochlea then pass messages to the brain so that we can 'hear' the sounds.

▼ Very tasty!

Your sense of taste is based on your tongue. Patches of receptors in certain areas on your tongue can taste things such as sweet, sour, salty and bitter. They produce messages that are passed to the brain. Taste works closely with smell.

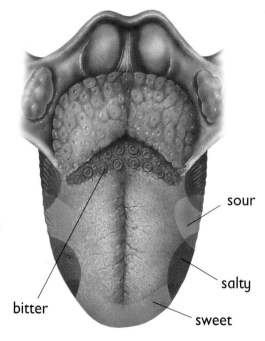

sour
salty
sweet
bitter

Sweet or salty?

Get someone to put a few grains of salt or sugar on your tongue. First on the tip, then the sides, then the back. See where you can taste the sweetness or saltiness.

▲ Touch and feel

Your fingertips contain lots of touch receptors. They are so sensitive that blind people can use their sense of touch to read Braille writing (tiny bumps on paper). You also have lots of touch receptors on your lips and around your eyes.

▲ Smelly signals

Tiny scent particles in the air pass to receptors in passages at the front of the skull. The receptors produce nerve signals that send 'smell' messages to the brain. Our sense of smell is poor compared to many animals.

Insects and spiders

Insects and spiders are very ancient animal groups. They have jointed legs and a tough skeleton on the outside of the body. Their bodies are divided into segments, which helps them move easily. The skeleton is made of chitin. Compared to other substances as light as this, chitin is one of the strongest materials known.

Word box

abdomen
largest part of an insect's body

antenna
found on insects' heads and used to feel and smell

▲ Growing and changing

As with certain other insects, butterflies change shape as they grow up. First, they hatch out as caterpillars. They cover themselves with a hard case – a pupa. Inside the pupa, a winged adult forms.

▲ Lots of legs

Spiders are not insects. Unlike insects, their bodies are divided into only two sections – the head and abdomen. They also have eight legs, and never have wings. Spiders are able to make a sticky, silky substance, which they use to catch insects to eat.

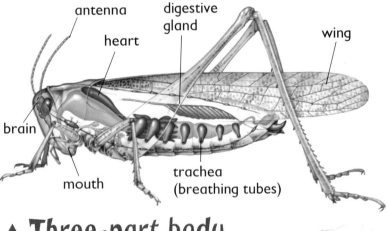

antenna
digestive gland
heart
wing
brain
mouth
trachea (breathing tubes)

▼ Working together

Many insects work together to supply food and protect their babies. These 'leaf-cutter' ants cut leaves and take them back to their nest. The leaves are used to grow a fungus that the ants eat.

▲ Three-part body

Most insects, like this grasshopper, are made up of three sections: head, thorax and abdomen. The legs and wings are attached to the thorax. The abdomen contains body parts for digesting food and reproducing.

Across the world, millions of computers are able to 'talk' to one another. This system is called the Internet. Information is mostly passed from computer to computer by telephone wires. The Internet lets people get hold of all kinds of information, in just a few seconds.

Word box

modem
device which lets computers send or receive information using phone lines

server
computer that holds information used by other computers

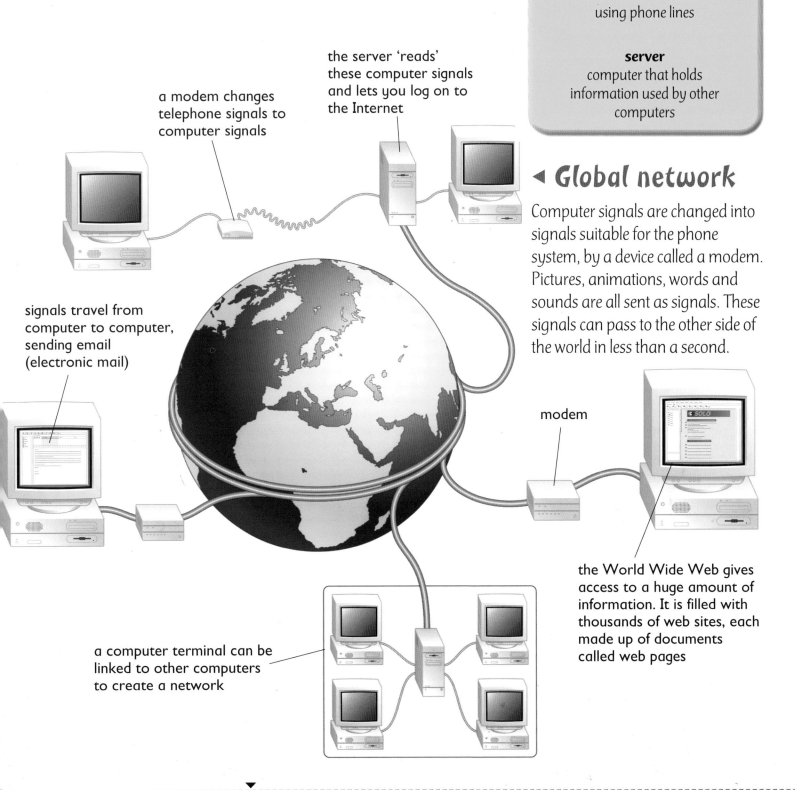

a modem changes telephone signals to computer signals

the server 'reads' these computer signals and lets you log on to the Internet

signals travel from computer to computer, sending email (electronic mail)

a computer terminal can be linked to other computers to create a network

modem

◄ Global network

Computer signals are changed into signals suitable for the phone system, by a device called a modem. Pictures, animations, words and sounds are all sent as signals. These signals can pass to the other side of the world in less than a second.

the World Wide Web gives access to a huge amount of information. It is filled with thousands of web sites, each made up of documents called web pages

Inventions

The first primitive person who chipped a flint to make a sharp knife made an important invention. So did the person who discovered how to make fire. Inventions can change the world, or they may just make our lives a bit easier. For example the zip seems like a simple invention, but it changed the way that people dressed all over the world.

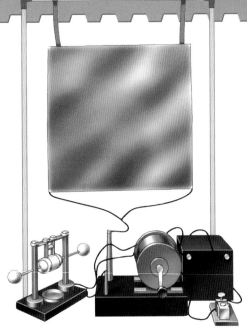

▲ Motor cars

The very first gasoline-powered cars (similar to the sort of cars we drive today) were invented in the early 1890s. This Ford family car first appeared in 1908. Its creator was Henry Ford. He was the first to use special machinery in order to make the cars more quickly and cheaply.

Word box

diagnose
find out what is making a person ill

electric current
a flow of electricity

wave
form of energy that is created by sound or light

▲ The first radio

An Italian man called Guglielmo Marconi made history with his invention – the radio. He worked out a way of using radio waves to send messages over long distances, in the 1890s-1900s.

► Zip-up

The zip was invented in 1891 by American engineer Whitcomb Judson. He used hooks and eyes that locked together by pulling a slide. This was later developed by using interlocking metal 'teeth' instead of hooks.

► Healthy inventions

Inventions in medicine help to improve health and save lives. This is an ECG (electrocardiograph) machine, used to diagnose heart problems. It picks up electric currents produced by the heartbeat and displays them on a screen.

Lasers

Light from a torch spreads out quickly and does not travel very far. Light from a piece of equipment called a laser, however, is very powerful. It can travel as far as the Moon, in a narrow beam. Lasers have many uses. They can be found in everyday household things such as CD and DVD players, or in factories, hospitals and even concerts.

▶ DVD lasers

A DVD (digital versatile disc) uses a tiny laser. This produces a very strong light beam. The beam scans (passes over) the DVDs surface. It 'reads' data (information) such as pictures, music and movies.

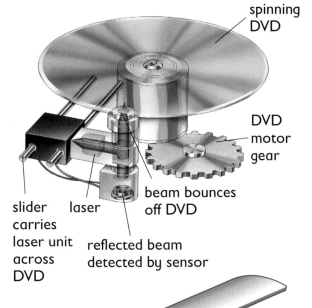

spinning DVD

DVD motor gear

beam bounces off DVD

slider carries laser unit across DVD

laser

reflected beam detected by sensor

▲ Lasers in industry

Laser light can contain enough energy to melt and cut through metal or almost any other substance. Factories that make clothes use computer-controlled lasers. They can cut out one shape in many thicknesses of fabric very quickly and accurately.

rays bounce off the mirrors at both ends, building up energy

mirror

half-mirror

laser light bursts from one end of the crystal

particles bounce around in ruby crystal

▼ Laser surgery

Lasers can be used to perform very delicate surgery, such as eye operations. Laser light does not spread out as normal light does. This means the beam can be very accurately directed and controlled.

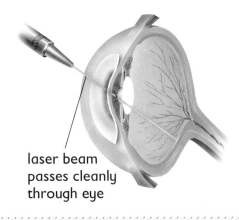

laser beam passes cleanly through eye

▲ How a laser works

Laser light is made by feeding energy, such as ordinary light or electricity, into a substance called the active medium. A rod of ruby crystal is the active medium in this laser. A powerful lamp causes the tiny particles inside the crystal to vibrate. The light builds up and is bounced between mirrors. The energy becomes so strong that it escapes from the laser as an intense beam.

Light

Light is a type of energy that you can see. It is usually produced by a very hot object such as a light bulb or a fire, and heat is released. But there are also 'cold' types of light – for example, the light produced by deep-sea fish or by glow-worms.

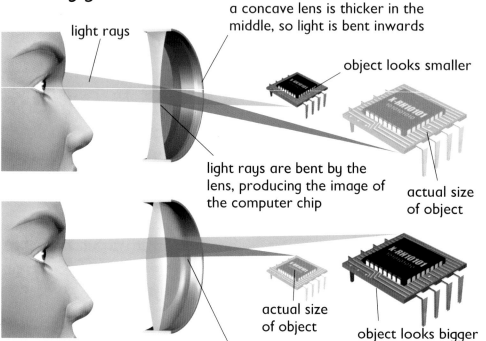

light rays

a concave lens is thicker in the middle, so light is bent inwards

object looks smaller

light rays are bent by the lens, producing the image of the computer chip

actual size of object

actual size of object

object looks bigger

a convex lens is thin in the middle, so light is bent outwards

▲ Bending light

When a straw is placed in water, it looks as though it is slightly bent. This is because light rays bend when they pass through water. This bending of rays is called refraction.

▲ Using lenses

Lenses are found in many optical (seeing) instruments, such as glasses, cameras and microscopes. The lenses are curved, so when light hits them, the rays bend. This makes an object look bigger or smaller than it really is.

▼ Mirror images

When light hits a very smooth surface such as a mirror, it reflects (bounces) off the surface. If it hits a mirror at an angle, it is reflected off at exactly the same angle.

Mirror fun

Take a shiny metal spoon, and look at your reflection in its bowl. Notice how your reflection gets larger and smaller, and even turns upside down! This is because light is working in a similar way to the diagram above, bouncing off the curved surface into your eyes.

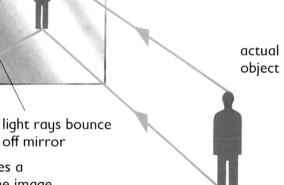

actual object

light rays bounce off mirror

the eye receives a reflection of the image

Light at work

Find out more:
Electricity ◄ Energy ◄ Lasers ◄ Light ◄

Light is essential for all kinds of things. Plants need the Sun's light for energy. We need light to grow food to eat and to be able to see around us. We make our own light with electricity or gas. In earlier times, people used fires, candles or oil for lighting.

◄ Cold light

Some animals produce an unusual kind of light that gives off no heat. Fireflies and glow-worms are insects that can make parts of their bodies glow with light. They do this to attract a mate. Some plants and moulds also glow in the dark.

▲ Stop or go?

Train drivers obey signal lights, just as drivers on the road obey traffic lights. Train signals show just two colours – red for stop and green for go. Road traffic lights have one extra colour – amber (yellow).

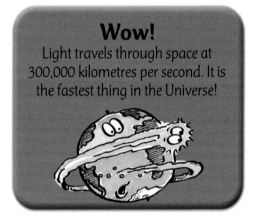

Wow!
Light travels through space at 300,000 kilometres per second. It is the fastest thing in the Universe!

▼ Light shows

Light can be used to create exciting displays. Laser light shows are often used at pop concerts. The beam from the laser is controlled by a computer, allowing it to make patterns in the air.

◄ Watch out!

For at least 2,000 years, lighthouses have used their flashing light to warn ships of danger. Lighthouses are tall, so that they can be seen from far away. Each lighthouse has its own pattern of light flashes, so that it can be easily identified. People used to work in lighthouses, but modern ones are automatic.

Machines

A machine is a device that helps us to carry out a certain job. A long stick used as a lever is the simplest type of machine – a modern aircraft is one of the most complicated types. Machines allow factories to produce the things we need to make our lives easier. We use machines in our homes, at school or for getting from place to place.

▲ Levers – the simplest machines

A long lever, tilted at a point called a fulcrum, can lift very heavy or tightly fixed objects. Here, a screwdriver is being used as a lever. The edge of the can is the fulcrum. The blade only needs to move a short distance to shift a very tight lid.

▶ Mega-mover

A bulldozer is a powerful machine for moving earth. A track or caterpillar track is kept running over a series of moving cogs. This spreads the weight of the machine over a large area, so it is less likely to skid or slip. The bulldozer pushes earth along with a steel blade.

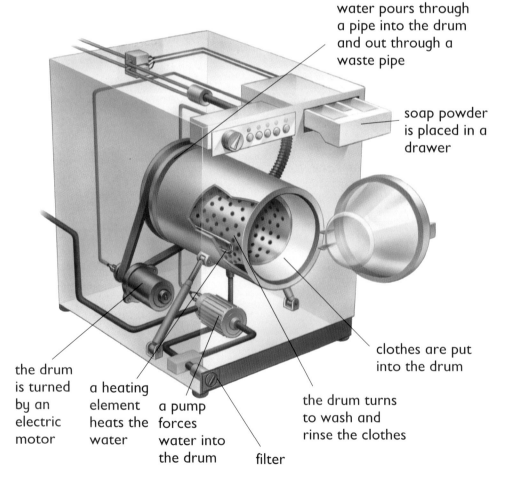

water pours through a pipe into the drum and out through a waste pipe

soap powder is placed in a drawer

clothes are put into the drum

the drum turns to wash and rinse the clothes

the drum is turned by an electric motor

a heating element heats the water

a pump forces water into the drum

filter

Word box

cog
teeth around the edge of a wheel

fulcrum
the point on which a lever is rested when it is used to shift heavy objects

◀ Household help

Washing clothes is one of the many household jobs that used to be done by hand. This required lots of time and effort. Washing machines wash, rinse and spin clothes in no time at all.

Machines in history

Find out more:
Engines ◄

Machines have been used for thousands of years. Very early machines did all kinds of jobs, from pumping water to attacking enemies. Some ancient machines, such as windmills and lock gates on canals, are still used today.

▲ Puffing Billy

This early steam engine helped Britain to begin the Industrial Revolution (when modern factories and industry began). Steam engines like this were used to move coal and iron. Similar coal-powered engines pulled the first passenger trains.

▲ War machine

This 'trebuchet' machine was used during medieval times for attacking stone castles. It had a long wooden arm with a sling. A heavy stone was placed in the sling and was then thrown towards the castle walls.

Wow!

The pyramids in Egypt were built about 4,500 years ago from huge blocks of stone. But no one really knows what machines were used to haul them into place.

▼ Natural forces

Windmills are machines that work by wind power. Once, they were used mainly for grinding grain, and may date back to AD600. Today, we use windmills to produce electricity. These windmills are often called 'wind turbines'.

◄ Raising water

This 'Archimedean screw' is named after the ancient Greek inventor, Archimedes. For thousands of years, it has been used to lift water from rivers to irrigate (bring water to) fields where crops grow. It is still used today in some Middle Eastern countries.

Magnets

Some metals are magnetic. 'Magnetic' means a metal can be attracted by a magnet or made into a magnet. This is how the compass works – it uses a magnetic needle that always swings to point north. Magnetism can also be produced by an electric circuit. This is useful because it can be switched on and off as needed.

▲ Curved magnets

The most common magnets are shaped like a horseshoe. The magnetic field is strongest between the arms of the horseshoe. Because of this magnetic field, a piece of iron or steel placed across the arms will stick to them.

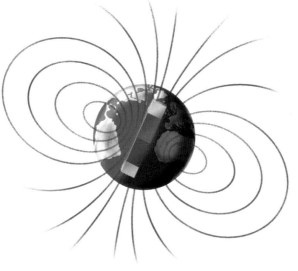

▲ Giant magnets

An 'electromagnet' is produced when electricity is passed through a coil of wire. It is only magnetic while the power is switched on. These magnets are used in industry to handle heavy steel objects.

Word box

electric circuit
a flow of electricity

magnetic field
area around a magnet where there is a magnetic force

Make a compass

You can easily make a simple compass. Take a small bar magnet (a straight magnet) and fix it to a piece of wood with sticky tape. Now float the wood in a dish of water and watch as the magnet slowly turns to point north and south. You can check that it is working properly with an ordinary magnetic compass.

▲ North and south

Deep down at the centre of the Earth is an enormous mass of iron. This acts as a huge magnet, which gives the Earth its magnetic field. The magnetic poles are not exactly at the North and South Poles. Also, they shift slightly every year.

◄ Pointing north

A compass is a tiny magnet, shaped like a needle and balanced so it can move easily. It turns to line itself up with the Earth's magnetic field, pointing to magnetic north. The invention of the compass was very important to early explorers.

Mammals

Mammals are warm-blooded animals. Mammal mothers give birth to live young, and feed them with their own milk. Most feed their unborn young through an organ called a placenta. Mammals vary a lot in appearance – humans, whales and mice are just three kinds. Inside, however, they are similar.

thumb · arm · furry body · second finger · third finger · foot · fourth finger · fifth finger · tail

skull · canine tooth · biceps and triceps muscles · radius · ulna · femur bone · shoulder blade · vertebrae (backbones) · hip joint

▲ Furry flyer

Bats are the only mammals that can fly. They are small and mouselike, and come out at night to find food. Their wings are made of skin, stretched between the fingers, arms and legs.

▲ Record-breaker

The blue whale is the largest animal that has ever lived. It can reach a length of 30 metres. Like all whales and dolphins, it spends all of its time in the water. Instead of fur, it has a layer of fat called blubber to keep it warm.

▲ Toolmakers

Chimpanzees are very clever mammals. These apes are our closest relatives. They have even invented tools. They poke sticks into ant or termite nests. They then pull the stick out, covered in insects for them to eat.

▲ Inside a mammal

Most mammals, like this bear, have a similar body structure. This includes fur or hair and four limbs. Female mammals also have mammary glands for feeding their young.

Word box

mammary glands
the part of a female mammal that produces milk for the young

vertebrae
row of small bones that make up the backbone of mammals

Materials in nature

Find out more:
Conservation ◀ Materials now ▶ Metals ▶
Recycling ▶

Every substance is made from material, or a combination of materials. The first materials used were natural. People wove fibres, built houses from straw and wood, and shaped stones and metals. We still use these materials today, but we must conserve and recycle them as much as we can, so they do not run out.

▼ Silk spinners

Silk is a strong, shiny fibre that is used to make cloth. It is made from the cocoons of caterpillars called silkworms. To make the cocoon, the silkworm produces a liquid that hardens into silk threads. At the same time it gives off a gum which sticks the threads of silk together.

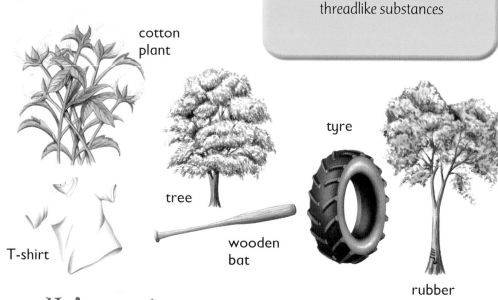

cotton plant

tree

tyre

T-shirt

wooden bat

rubber tree

silkworm

▲ Using nature

A large number of everyday materials are made from plants, such as cotton, wood and rubber. Some everyday items are shown here, next to the plant that was used to make them.

▶ Simple straw

Natural materials such as straw have been used to build houses since ancient times. Straw consists of dried stems of grains such as wheat, oats and barley. This Chinese hut has a thatched roof made of straw and is held up with poles and beams of wood.

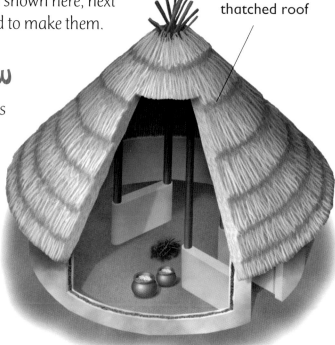

thatched roof

Which material?

Look at the list of items below. Which natural material is each commonly made from?

a. kitchen table
b. pair of socks
c. wellington boots

a. wood b. cotton c. rubber
answers

Materials now

Many materials we use today are natural, but synthetic (chemically made) ones are also very common. Plastic, steel and glass are examples of synthetic materials. Sometimes materials can be a mixture of both natural and synthetic – these are often used to make clothing.

▶ Strong and light

The main body of a racing car is made from carbon fibre. Carbon fibres are silky threads of pure carbon that are used to reinforce (strengthen) plastics. This mixture creates a light but very strong material.

main body of the car made from carbon fibre

▼ Body-builder

Titanium is a metal stronger than steel but half its weight. Also, it doesn't wear away easily. It is used in aircraft and spacecraft. Titanium and plastic parts also replace human body parts, such as knees and hips, when they wear out.

▲ Mixing it up

Plastics can be mixed with natural fibres to make strong fabrics for sails, parachutes and hot-air balloons. Nylon, acrylic and polyester are types of plastic which are spun together with cotton or wool.

Wow!

Glass can be specially treated so that it becomes extra tough – strong enough to be made into bulletproof windows!

◄ Useful plastic

Plastics are synthetic materials made mainly from the substances in petroleum, or crude oil. They can be made into different shapes by melting them or by changing them chemically. There are many kinds of plastics, all of which are usually strong, waterproof and long-lasting.

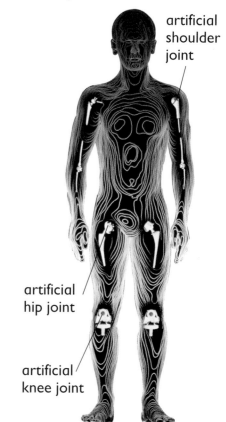

artificial shoulder joint

artificial hip joint

artificial knee joint

Measuring

You can measure many things roughly just by looking at them or feeling their weight in your hand. But to measure accurately you need special tools such as rulers and scales. Measuring is vital so that we can make things properly. It also means we know exactly what we are buying or using.

lights swing at level 3

windows breaking at level 5

chimneys topple at level 6

◀ Balancing act

Simple scales work by balancing various weights against the object you want to weigh. A heavy object needs more weights to balance it. These scales are mostly being replaced by digital ones, which are more accurate.

▼ Hot and cold

Thermometers are used to measure temperature. Traditional ones, such as this, are filled with mercury. This shows the temperature as it moves along a glass tube. Mercury can be very poisonous, so modern thermometers are electronic. They show the temperature as figures on a small screen.

Word box

DIY
'do it yourself' jobs around the home, such as putting up shelves

mercury
a heavy, silvery metal used in thermometers, which is liquid

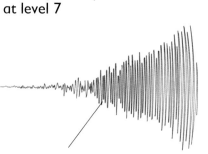

bridges and buildings collapse at level 7

the Richter scale

▼ Tape it!

Short distances are easily measured with a tape measure. This usually has metres, centimetres and millimetres on one side, and feet and inches on the other. Tape measures are used in dressmaking, DIY and by builders and surveyors measuring buildings.

▲ Measuring nature

It is not easy to measure natural forces such as earthquakes. The Richter scale measures the strength of the shockwaves and energy produced by an earthquake.

Medicines

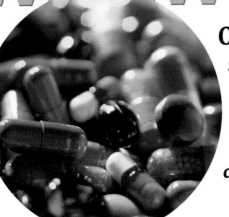

Our body can usually look after itself very well, but sometimes things go wrong. Some of the thousands of chemicals in the body may get out of balance. Perhaps a part wears out. Germs may attack and cause disease. Medicines are designed to put these things right and to make us feel better.

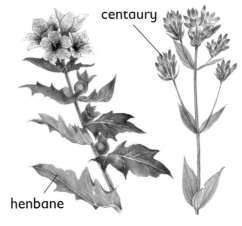

centaury

henbane

▲ Pills and capsules

Most medicines are swallowed as tablets or capsules. These are specially designed to dissolve properly in the stomach so they will be absorbed, or taken into your body. They are made in all kinds of colours, so people do not mix them up.

Word box

anaesthetic
a drug that takes away any feeling, so that no pain is felt during an operation

antibiotics
medicines used to treat illnesses caused by bacteria

vaccination
medicine given to a person to stop them getting a harmful disease

▲ Nature's cures

Plants have been used as medicines for thousands of years. Some, like henbane, can be very poisonous unless they are used in tiny amounts. Bitter-tasting centaury is still used as a tonic and to reduce fevers.

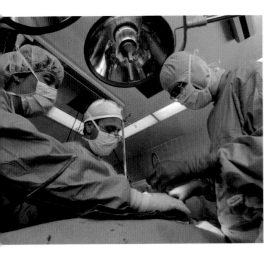

▼ Self-protection

People are vaccinated by being given doses of a dead or harmless germ. The body thinks that these are dangerous, so it produces lots of substances called antibodies. These prevent you from getting the real disease later on.

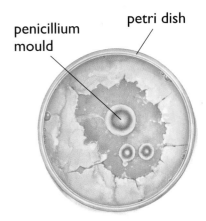

petri dish

penicillium mould

▲ Body repair

Doctors called surgeons repair damage and remove diseased parts during operations. The invention of substances called anaesthetics meant that people could have operations without pain. Heart and liver transplants are among the most complicated types of surgery.

▲ Bacteria-killer

Penicillin is an antibiotic that has saved the lives of millions of people. It first came from a mould – like the blue mould seen on stale bread. This was accidentally found to be able to kill bacteria.

Metals are mostly shiny, strong materials that are solid at room temperature. They can be hammered into different shapes. They can also be shaped by being melted and poured into a mould. Metals have been used since earliest times and have allowed modern civilization to develop.

▲ Save and reuse

It is mostly cheaper and less wasteful to reuse metal than to dig up more ore and process it. Metals such as old drinks cans, cars and other waste can be recycled (reused). They are crushed into blocks and sent off to be melted down again.

Word scramble

Unscramble these words to find the names of different kinds of metal or alloy:

a. NIRO

b. ZENORB

c. POPERC

d. NIT

answers
a. iron b. bronze c. copper d. tin

▲ Metal money

Coins are stamped out of strips of metal such as copper, silver or mixtures of metals called alloys. Coins are heavy, so notes are used for large amounts of money.

Word box

alloy
a mixture of metals, or a metal and a non-metal

ore
a mixture of different substances, of which metal is one

► The age of bronze

Bronze is an alloy (mix) of copper and tin. Copper is a very soft metal, but adding tin makes it much harder. This was discovered thousands of years ago, during the 'Bronze Age', when people made bronze axes that still survive today.

► Iron strength

The Eiffel Tower, in Paris, France, was built for an exhibition in 1898. It was only meant to last for a few years, but it is still standing. This tower is made of wrought iron, a type of metal that is both tough and flexible. Most modern towers are made from steel, which is iron mixed with carbon.

Microscopes

A microscope lets us see tiny things that we cannot see with our own eyes, such as bacteria. It works by using groups of lenses. Lenses are made from see-through materials and are shaped to make things larger or clearer for us. Electron microscopes allow us to see even smaller things, such as viruses. Studying their structure helps us produce treatments for the diseases they cause.

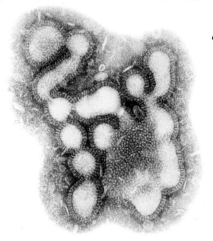

▲ The flu virus

This is the flu virus, viewed under an electron microscope. Chemicals, called fixatives, preserve the viruses so that they are not smashed by the microscope's electron beam. This allows the virus to be examined.

Word box

virus
the simplest form of life; viruses live inside a cell, so the body finds it hard to attack them

▼ 3D pictures

This piece of hair is being viewed under a binocular microscope. A binocular microscope has two eyepieces and two objective lenses. It gives a 3D view with depth.

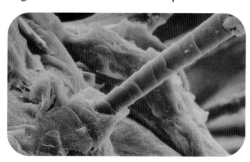

electricity supply

electron gun

air removed

electrons released

coils of wire control beam

electron beam

beam passes through hole

beam scans to and fro

object

flash detector screen

▲ Particle power

An electron microscope is very powerful. It can magnify an object (make it look larger) by millions of times. It works by firing special particles called electrons at the object. The electrons bounce off the object onto a viewing screen.

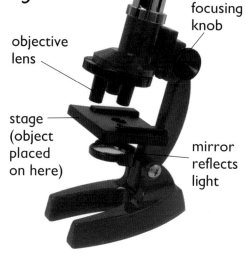

eyepiece

focusing knob

objective lens

stage (object placed on here)

mirror reflects light

▲ Using lenses

'Compound optical' microscopes use two or more lenses to make images up to 2,000 times bigger. An objective lens bends light rays to enlarge the object. An eyepiece lens then lets you see the final image.

Make a microscope

Use a magnifying glass to look at something small. Note how big the glass makes it look. Now use another magnifying glass, held under the first. The image looks even bigger. As you move the lenses up and down the size of the image changes. It will become sharp or blurred. This is what happens inside a microscope as the views are focused.

Minerals

When metals and other useful materials are dug out of the ground, they are in the form of minerals. Minerals are formed and reformed when molten rock (magma) pushes up from below the Earth's crust. It then cools and becomes solid. Minerals are mined (taken from the Earth) by digging deep holes, or they are taken from riverbeds and seabeds.

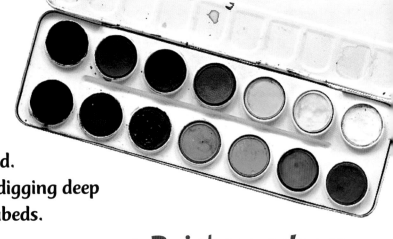

quartz crystal

Word box

ceramics
objects shaped from clay that have been baked at a high temperature

compound
substance containing more than one type of element

▲ Crystal clear

Minerals often form as crystals. This is when minerals cool slowly. Quartz is a compound of silicon and oxygen. Quartz has many uses, such as measuring time in watches and clocks.

▼ Clay for pots

Clay is used for making pots, bricks and other ceramics. It is found in most types of soil, and is made up of a group of minerals called silicates. Clay is also used in farming – it helps soil to keep in the minerals that plants need to grow (see 'Deep in the soil').

▲ Rainbow colours

Some minerals have bright colours and are sometimes used as pigments (coloured substances) to give paints, dyes and inks their colour. Iron oxide, for example, gives the colours red and yellow.

▼ Deep in the soil

Soil contains minerals which supply nutrients (goodness) to green plants, helping them grow. The plants take in, or absorb, these minerals through their roots.

the tree's roots take in minerals from the soil

Moon

Our Moon is a small ball of rock, travelling around the Earth. It is the closest natural object to us in the Solar System. Because it moves regularly round the Earth, the Moon has always been used to measure time. It also controls the rise and fall of the tides.

high tides occur at the same time on opposite sides of the Earth

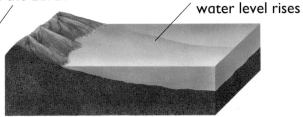
at high tide the water level rises

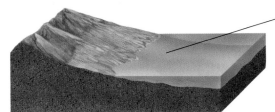
at low tide the water level goes down again

▲ Where is it from?

Scientists still do not know exactly where the Moon came from. Most think that the Moon formed from rocky bits and pieces thrown out when a huge object crashed into Earth. These bits and pieces joined together in a single mass to form the Moon.

Word box

meteor
a piece of rock passing through space

orbit
curved path that the Moon takes around the Earth

▲ The Earth's tides

As the Moon orbits the Earth and the Earth spins, its gravity pulls all the time at the Earth's surface. This makes the oceans move towards the Moon. The surge follows the path of the Moon. Tides rise as the Moon passes over. They fall as water is pulled towards other parts of the Earth. It is rather like water sloshing from one end of a bath to the other.

► Man on the Moon

Twelve people have made the very dangerous journey to the Moon, and walked on its surface. Its surface is a mass of rock, covered with dust caused by meteors crashing into it. Gravity is weak so it is easy to walk and jump, even in a heavy space suit.

Moon-gazer!

Use a pair of binoculars to look at the surface of the Moon. You may just be able to see some of the huge craters (pits) on its surface. You can sometimes see these more clearly when there is a crescent Moon, with sunlight hitting it at an angle. Never look at the Sun directly, especially with binoculars – it could damage your eyes.

Numbers

Numbers are how we store information about amounts. They also let us calculate (do sums). In the simplest type of calculation, we use our fingers to help us count. Modern computers can make trillions of calculations in just one second.

▲ Computer bits

Computers use a code called the binary code to make calculations. This code uses only two numbers: 0 and 1. Each 0 or 1 is called a 'bit', short for binary digit. The 'bits' combine in different ways to make letters, symbols and numbers. Each combination of 'bits' is called a 'byte'.

▲ Fun with numbers

Numbers can be fun! Many games use numbers to count scores and to have fun with your skill and luck. Card and dice games are major number-users. They have been played for hundreds of years and are still popular.

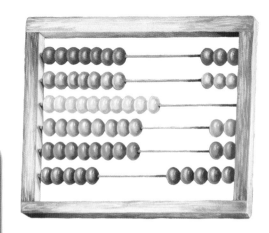

Wow!

Any number between 10 and 99, when written three times, can be divided by seven to give a whole number as a result. For example, 121212 divided by 7 = 17316

▲ Round the world

Many civilizations invented systems of numbers. Most ancient systems did not use the number zero. This made counting hard. Arabic numbers are now the main system, because they are easy to use.

▲ Ancient adding

The abacus is a very ancient adding machine. It uses a series of sliding beads to count, and it is still used today in some countries. It looks very simple, but with practice people can add large sums really quickly.

Oceans and seas

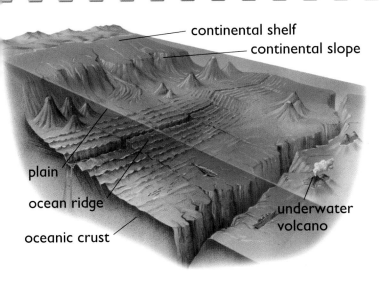

continental shelf
continental slope
plain
ocean ridge
oceanic crust
underwater volcano

Nearly three quarters of the Earth's surface is covered by sea. The oceans' currents are flowing all the time and circulate the world's sea water. These currents greatly affect our climate and the amount of rainfall over land areas.

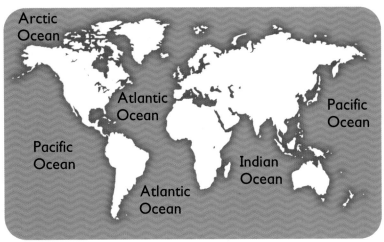

Arctic Ocean
Atlantic Ocean
Pacific Ocean
Pacific Ocean
Indian Ocean
Atlantic Ocean

▲ Underwater world

The seabed is not flat – it contains similar features to the land. There may be huge mountain ranges, totally underwater. Deep valleys and wide plains may be found on the seabed. There is also a broad ledge around all the continents. This is called the continental shelf.

▼ Icy waters

If temperatures rise slightly, icecaps at the North and South Poles start to melt. This causes huge icebergs to break off. Some icebergs weigh thousands of tonnes. Nearly all of their bulk is under the water.

Word box

current
movement of water through the ocean or sea

icecap
large mass of ice

sea
small area or edge around an ocean

▲ Earth's oceans

There are four oceans on Earth. The largest is the Pacific, which covers one-third of the planet's surface. Currents circulate around all the world's oceans. They spread materials washed into the sea from rivers. This helps to feed all sea life.

► Giant waves

In parts of the world where earthquakes are common, an undersea quake can make huge waves sweep over the land. These are called tsunamis. They can cause tremendous damage.

Photography

Photography is the process of making pictures by using light. Photographs are made using cameras. Like the human eye, some cameras take in light from an object, and record this image on film. Images can also be produced in digital cameras, which, instead of using film, are processed in computers.

▲ Digital photos

Ordinary cameras record pictures on film, but the modern digital camera records them in electronic form. The pictures can be loaded into a computer, printed or viewed on screen. The digital image can be changed in any way you want.

Wow!

Some cameras can see in the dark. They make a black and white picture by picking up the faintest traces of light from the stars or the Moon.

▼ Get snappy!

Modern automatic cameras do most of the work for you! They control the amount of light falling onto the film, the size of the image, and how long the light falls on the film (the shutter speed). With the older manual camera, you would have to make all these calculations and adjustments yourself.

▼ Old times

The first photographs were made in the 1840s. Early photography used a different method for printing. Instead of being printed in black and white, the pictures came out in a brownish colour called sepia.

► Watch out!

Digital cameras are now made so small that they can be fitted into a watch. Wrist camera watches record images which can then be transferred to a computer and viewed in full colour.

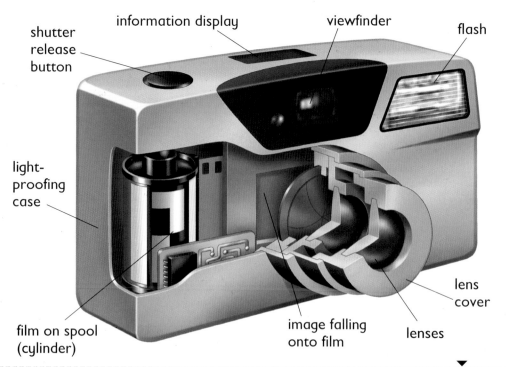

shutter release button — information display — viewfinder — flash — light-proofing case — film on spool (cylinder) — image falling onto film — lenses — lens cover

Planets

Planets are large bodies of rock, metal and gas that travel round a star. Nine planets, including Earth, orbit our own star, the Sun. The Earth is a small planet, while planets such as Jupiter and Saturn are far bigger. Earth is the only planet that is the right distance from the Sun for any life to exist here.

Word box

orbit
travel round

star
a ball of very hot gas

► Saturn's rings

Saturn is often called the Ringed Planet. It is surrounded by flat rings that can be clearly seen through a telescope. They are only one kilometre thick – the planet's width is 60,000 kilometres. Although the rings look smooth, they are made up of millions of pieces of ice and rock. These orbit the planet and stretch thousands of kilometres out into space.

▼ Our Solar System

Together with the Sun, various moons and lumps of rock, the planets make up the Solar System. Mercury, Venus, Earth and Mars are known as the 'inner planets' because they are closest to the Sun. Jupiter, Saturn, Uranus, Neptune and Pluto lie farther away, so are known as the 'outer planets'. Outer planets take much longer for each orbit – Pluto takes 248 of our years.

Sun

Venus Mercury

Earth

Moon

Mars

Jupiter

Saturn

Uranus

Neptune

Pluto

Plant kingdom

Like the animal kingdom, the plant kingdom includes a huge range of living things. Unlike animals, plants can make their own food, from water and air. Using photosynthesis, they change sunlight into sugar. This gives them energy for life and growth.

Word box

classify
divide living things into groups to make them easier to study

photosynthesis
a process plants use to turn energy from sunlight into food

► Plants galore!

Scientists 'classify' the many types of plants, shown here. They are usually grouped by comparing the structure of their stems and leaves, how they take in food and water and how they reproduce.

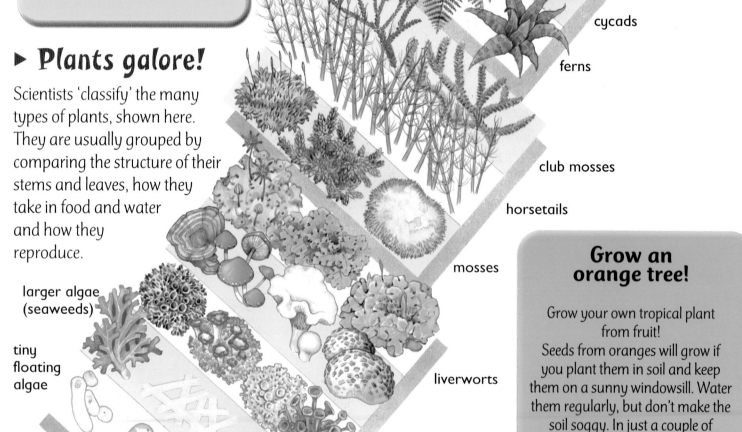

broadleaved trees and bushes, flowers and herbs

grasses, lilies and palms

gingkos

conifers

cycads

ferns

club mosses

horsetails

mosses

liverworts

lichens

larger algae (seaweeds)

tiny floating algae

Grow an orange tree!

Grow your own tropical plant from fruit!
Seeds from oranges will grow if you plant them in soil and keep them on a sunny windowsill. Water them regularly, but don't make the soil soggy. In just a couple of weeks, a tiny orange tree will begin to grow.

Plant life

The way a plant lives depends on many things, such as climate and soil. The simplest plants, such as algae (*'algee'*), do not even need soil. They grow in ponds, lakes and oceans. Other plants, such as cacti (*'cacteye'*), grow in dry deserts. They can live without water for long periods of time.

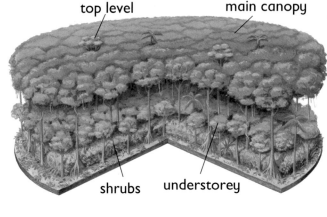

emergent top level

main canopy

shrubs

understorey

◄ Desert plants

Cacti are specially adapted to stop them from losing too much water in the hot sun. They are often covered with spikes, to prevent animals from eating them.

▲ Layers and layers

In tropical rainforests, different plants grow at different heights, depending on the amount of light available. Sunlight passes through the highest trees to a more even layer – the main canopy. This thick layer blocks out most of the light, so that only a few plants, creepers or bushes, can grow underneath.

Word box

canopy
layer of plants in the rainforest 'roof'

understorey
layer of plants in the rainforest found below the main canopy

▲ Going up...

Weather conditions get colder and windier high up in the mountains. On lower slopes, conifer trees such as pines and firs grow. Higher up, above what is called the tree-line, it is too cold for trees. Instead, shrubs, grasses and tiny flowers grow.

► Living together

Scientists are always trying to find out more about how plants and humans live together. *Biosphere 2* was an enclosed living space where people stayed for a while. They experimented with growing many types of plants in different conditions.

Pollution

Humans do all kinds of things that produce waste materials, and these pollute our world. Smoke from factories damages the air. Waste from factories, homes and similar places pours into rivers and is carried out to sea. Cars and other vehicles produce huge amounts of pollution in many of the world's cities, even making it hard to breathe.

▼ Self-destruction

We are beginning to see the damage we are doing to the world around us. New filters and chemicals called catalysts can reduce dangerous fumes. Many organizations are now working to stop us doing further harm. But we still have a long way to go.

Wow!

If pollution continues at the current rate, 30 to 50 per cent of all living species may be extinct by the middle of the 21st century.

▲ Water pollution

Factory and human waste are the usual causes of river pollution. These waste materials take oxygen from the water. This kills fish and other water life.

factories pump out chemicals that escape into the atmosphere, making rainwater acidic. This can kill trees and damage soil

cutting down trees destroys forests and wildlife

factories make huge piles of waste

rubbish is dumped in rivers or landfill sites

exhaust fumes from traffic can make it hard to breathe

Recycling

Find out more:
Conservation ◄ Materials in nature ◄ Materials now ◄ Metals ◄
Pollution ◄

Pollution is less of a problem when waste materials are reused instead of being thrown away. Glass is easily melted down for recycling. Paper can also be recycled, saving millions of trees. Today there are all kinds of schemes that help people to recycle things.

▼ How we recycle

Waste material from homes and factories is taken to recycling centres. Useful materials are picked out and stored, ready to be changed back into many of the things we use every day.

Recycle it!

Keep an eye on the things that your family throws away each day – but don't start sorting through yucky rubbish! Try to think of things that could be taken to your local recycling centre, such as paper, plastic, cans and bottles. As much as half of your family's waste can be recycled.

▲ Farming trees

Instead of destroying forest trees for wood and paper, it is better to grow trees specially, on big plantations like this one. Fast-growing trees are used. They are cut down as soon as they reach a useful size and are quickly replaced with new trees.

1. used glass or plastic bottles, aluminium cans and newspapers are collected from recycling centres

2. the objects are recycled to make raw materials

3. the raw materials are reused to make new bottles, cans and paper

▲ Sorting it out

Useful rubbish from ordinary homes needs to be sorted out first by hand, before it goes to the recycling centre.

Reptiles

**Reptiles are cold-blooded creatures that usually have dry, scaly skin.
They cannot produce their own body heat, so they often lie in the sun to warm up.
The main kinds of reptile are lizards, snakes, turtles, tortoises,
crocodiles and alligators. Reptiles are descended from very
ancient animals – the dinosaurs were reptiles.**

▼ Open wide!

Snakes hunt live food. Some can eat animals that appear to be far
too big to swallow. Snakes have special jaws. This rat snake is
crushing a rat. It will then open its jaws very wide so it can
swallow the rat head-first.

▲ Turtle babies

Turtles lay eggs, like most reptiles.
The turtle spends most of its time in
water, but comes onto dry land to
lay its eggs. Reptile eggs are soft
and leathery, unlike the hard, brittle
eggs that birds lay.

Wow!

The South American anaconda
snake can swallow animals as large
as a deer, antlers included!

▶ Tough caimans

The caiman is a close relative of the
alligator. It has the toughest skin of
any alligator or crocodile. There are
five species, and all of them are
found in Central and South
America. They live in fresh water,
such as rivers and lakes.

Rocks

The hard surface of the Earth is made of rock. Many of these rocks were made deep inside the Earth, where it is very hot. Other rocks formed from mud and sand, under enormous pressure (force) and heat.

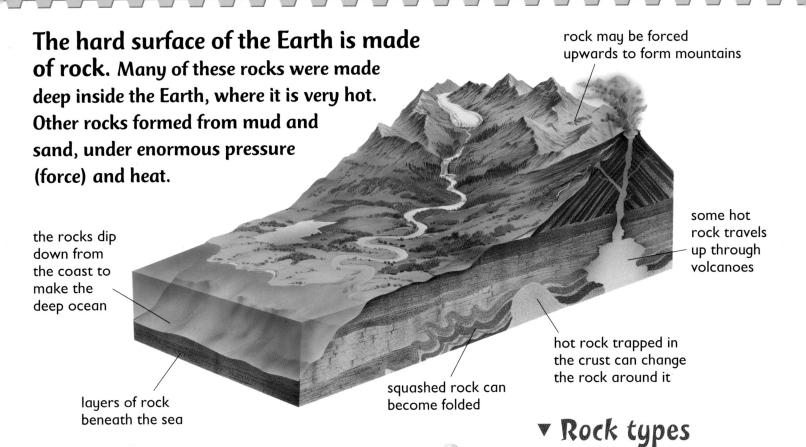

rock may be forced upwards to form mountains

the rocks dip down from the coast to make the deep ocean

some hot rock travels up through volcanoes

layers of rock beneath the sea

squashed rock can become folded

hot rock trapped in the crust can change the rock around it

▲ Above and below

Layers of rock form underground, in the Earth's crust. Some of the rock may be changed by great heat found deep inside the Earth. Rock can also be crushed and folded to form features such as mountain ranges.

chalk forms at the bottom of the seabed

limestone is made from seashells

mudstone is made from squashed mud

▼ Rock types

There are many different types of rock. Their appearance, colour and structure depend on how they were formed. Some form as a result of volcanic activity. Others are produced from material that is carried by rivers and deposited (dropped) in the sea.

► Wearing away

Strong desert winds carry grains of sand that erode (wear away) the rocks. Soft rocks may be worn into strange shapes like this arch. The sea and freezing weather can both wear away soft cliffs and rocks.

Sciences

Science is the study of everything about us, from the living world to the stars and planets.
Sciences, such as astronomy and mathematics, are many centuries old. Other sciences, such as computer science, did not exist until 60 years ago. Science never stands still — new things are being discovered all the time.

▶ Which science?

There are many different kinds of science. Here are a few examples. All aim to examine a certain part of the world or Universe, and find an explanation. Many scientists work in more than one area, such as biochemistry (biology and chemistry).

Biology
How animals and plants live, grow, produce young and find food.
Why are leaves green?

Chemistry
What things are made from, and how they behave in different ways.
What is salt made of?

Physics
How the Universe works, how and why things happen to it.
How does an aircraft fly?

Geology
How the Earth was made, its structure, rocks and minerals.
How do mountains form?

Astronomy
The study of the Universe, its planets, stars and galaxies.
When did the Universe begin?

Archaeology
The study of ancient remains, such as skulls and bones.
How tall were the ancient Egyptians?

◀ Scientists at work

Some scientists work in laboratories. Here, they start with an idea, or theory, which asks how something will react in a certain situation. They then carry out experiments, or tests, to see what will happen. The results — what happens at the end — are written down and studied. Finally, the scientist thinks of reasons, or conclusions, for why certain things occurred during the experiment.

Scientists

Find out more:
Chemicals ◄ Sciences ◄

The first true scientists were people who would not accept traditional or everyday ideas about how things worked, but wanted to find out for themselves. Their new ideas were often disliked by other people, who were used to thinking in a certain way.

Word box

anatomy
the human body

BC (Before Christ)
the years before the birth of Christ

1500 — 1500s — 1550 — 1600s — 1600 — 1650 — 1700

▼ Leonardo da Vinci (1452–1519)
An Italian artist who designed many devices, including a type of aircraft (see below). He also made detailed scientific drawings of the human anatomy.

▼ Isaac Newton (1642–1727)
An English mathematician who devised the laws of motion and gravity. He also built the first reflecting telescope.

▲ Galileo Galilei (1564–1642)
An Italian astronomer who invented the first thermometer, and proved that the planets move around the Sun.

◄▼ Great minds

This chart shows just a few of the many scientists who have made ground-breaking discoveries in the last 500 years. Of course, many brilliant thinkers existed before this time. Around 235BC, for example, a Greek mathematician called Archimedes made several important scientific discoveries. These included how levers work and why an object floats.

1700 — 1700s — 1750 — 1800s — 1800 — 1850 — 1900 — 1900s — 1950 — 2000

▼ Michael Faraday (1791–1867)
An English scientist who invented many electrical machines, like the motor and the dynamo.

◄ Albert Einstein (1879–1955)
German-born physicist who made discoveries about space and time, and about nuclear energy and the atom bomb.

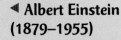

▲ Antoine Lavoisier (1743–1794)
A French scientist who discovered water was made of oxygen and hydrogen. He began the modern system of naming chemicals.

► Alexander Fleming (1881–1955)
A Scottish doctor who discovered penicillin, a substance important as an antibiotic (medicine used to treat illnesses).

Solids, liquids and gases

Find out more:
Air ◀ Atoms and molecules ◀

Most substances exist in different forms.
Temperature and pressure play a major role. For example, most metals are solid at normal temperatures. However, they become liquid if they are heated strongly. The gas carbon dioxide becomes solid, like snow, if it is cold enough. Nitrogen gas turns into liquid when very cold.

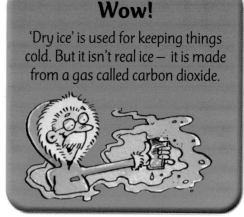

Wow!
'Dry ice' is used for keeping things cold. But it isn't real ice — it is made from a gas called carbon dioxide.

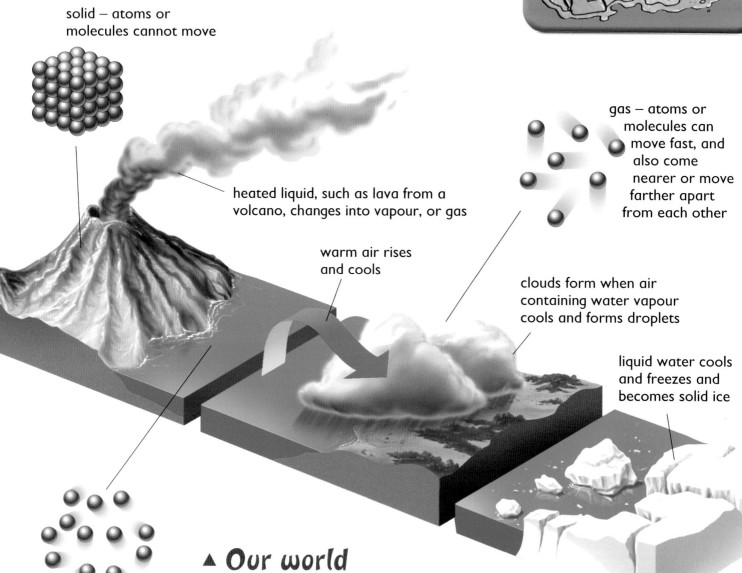

solid – atoms or molecules cannot move

heated liquid, such as lava from a volcano, changes into vapour, or gas

warm air rises and cools

gas – atoms or molecules can move fast, and also come nearer or move farther apart from each other

clouds form when air containing water vapour cools and forms droplets

liquid water cools and freezes and becomes solid ice

liquid – atoms or molecules can move or flow but they stay the same distance apart

▲ Our world

Everything around us is either a solid, liquid or gas, made up of units called atoms. Solid matter, like a volcano's rocks, is made up of tightly packed molecules that cannot move about. Liquids, such as water, contain molecules that are more widely spaced, and can move about more easily. Gases, such as air, are made up of molecules that can move about freely.

Sound

Sound is caused by the vibrations of air or any other material, including water. You can feel these vibrations, called waves, if you put your hand on the speaker of a radio that is playing loudly. In space, there are no particles (tiny objects) to carry the vibration, so sound cannot travel in this way.

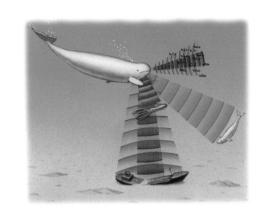

▼ How do we hear sound?

The outer ear collects sounds in the air, like a funnel. From here, sounds pass through a tube called the ear canal, and then to the ear drum. Sounds make the ear drum and tiny bones in the middle ear vibrate. These bones pass the sound to the cochlea, in the inner ear. Here, nerve cells change the vibrations into messages that travel to the brain, so we recognize what we are hearing.

▲ Whale 'sonar'

Whales and dolphins make high-pitched squeaks, clicks and whistles. These bounce off the seabed and off the shoals (groups) of fish that whales eat. This helps whales to build up a 'sound picture' of their surroundings and also to find food.

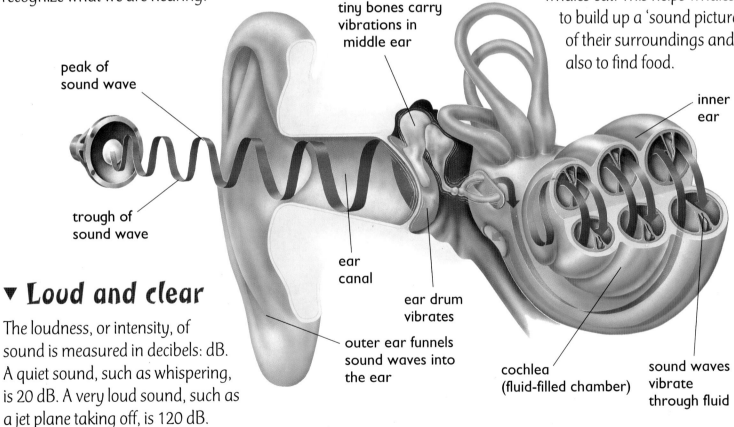

peak of sound wave

trough of sound wave

tiny bones carry vibrations in middle ear

inner ear

ear canal

ear drum vibrates

outer ear funnels sound waves into the ear

cochlea (fluid-filled chamber)

sound waves vibrate through fluid

▼ Loud and clear

The loudness, or intensity, of sound is measured in decibels: dB. A quiet sound, such as whispering, is 20 dB. A very loud sound, such as a jet plane taking off, is 120 dB.

talking 40 dB

jet taking off 120 dB

motorbike 70 dB

vacuum cleaner 60 dB

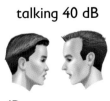

whispering 20 dB

Space travel

People dreamed about space travel for centuries, but it only began in the second half of the 1900s. It was made possible by the development of powerful rockets. People sent into space are called astronauts. However, space exploration today tends to be done by robots.

▲ Working in space

Space stations are scientific laboratories, 'parked' above the Earth. Astronauts get there by space shuttle or rocket. They may stay for many months before coming home. The stations run on electricity. They make this from light energy collected from the Sun.

▶ Sound asleep

Due to lack of gravity, astronauts float about in their space station. So, in order to sleep, they get into a special sleeping bag that can be fixed down securely.

eSa

Wow!

People in space grow taller – by up to 5 cm. There is no gravity to pull them down, so their spines are allowed to stretch!

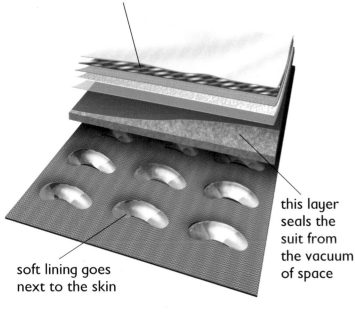

outer layers protect from the fierce heat of the Sun

this layer seals the suit from the vacuum of space

soft lining goes next to the skin

◀▶ Special suits

When astronauts leave the safety of their craft, they need to wear spacesuits. These protect them from extreme heat and cold. The spacesuit has several layers. It has an air supply to help the astronauts breathe, and fluid is pumped through the suit to keep the astronauts at a comfortable temperature.

Spacecraft

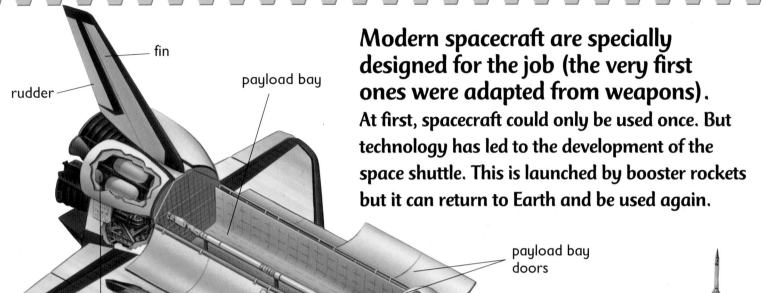

fin

rudder

payload bay

payload bay doors

flightdeck

rocket engines

Modern spacecraft are specially designed for the job (the very first ones were adapted from weapons). At first, spacecraft could only be used once. But technology has led to the development of the space shuttle. This is launched by booster rockets but it can return to Earth and be used again.

Word box

capsule
small cabin that is carried into space by rockets

manned
with people on board

satellite
spacecraft that circles the Earth; some are used to help send telephone and TV signals

▲ Space shuttles

US space shuttles take humans and cargo into orbit around Earth (to circle around Earth), and then return home again. Coming back to Earth, the shuttle is the world's heaviest glider (flying without power). It comes down fast, and needs a parachute to slow down on the runway.

Saturn V moon rocket

Energiya launcher/ Buran shuttle

► Blast off!

To blast into space, a rocket has to travel 40 times faster than a jumbo jet. If it went any slower, gravity would pull it back to Earth. Rockets are used to send manned capsules and satellites into orbit and spacecraft to the Moon.

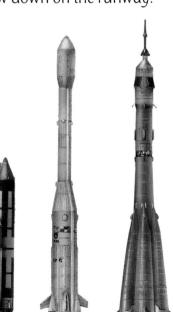

Titan 3   *Ariane*   *Vostok*

Stars

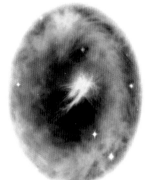

Stars are huge bodies floating in space. Our own Sun is a star. Many stars are easily seen in the night sky. They keep twinkling because of nuclear explosions that continue for millions of years. Other stars have almost burned out and cannot be seen from Earth.

▲ Supernova

Sometimes a star explodes into a supernova. This destroys the star and burns brilliantly for about a week. The supernova then turns into a huge cloud of gas and dust.

1. clumps of gas start to shrink into tight balls

2. the gas spirals round as it is pulled inwards

3. new star starts making heat and light, but is still hidden by cloud of dust and gas

4. dust and gas are blown away to reveal shining star

Word box

hemisphere
the upper (Northern) and lower (Southern) hemispheres are the two halves of the Earth. They are separated by an imaginary line – the Equator.

◀ Birth of a star

Stars probably formed from clouds of hot gases that were produced when the Universe formed. Gravity drew these gases and dust into huge balls in space. Great pressure and heat then set off a reaction to power the stars and produce heat and light.

▶ Star maps

On a clear night, you can see huge numbers of stars in the sky. Some of them form patterns that are easily recognizable and have been given names. Someone living in the southern half of the world sees different patterns to someone in the north. People once used the stars' positions to guide them on long ocean voyages.

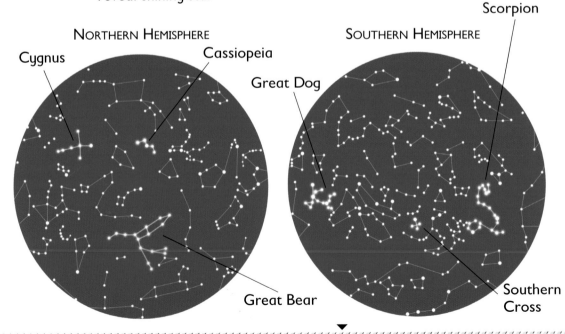

NORTHERN HEMISPHERE

Cygnus

Cassiopeia

Great Bear

SOUTHERN HEMISPHERE

Scorpion

Great Dog

Southern Cross

Sun

Our Sun is a star that is about 150,000,000 kilometres from the Earth. It is around 1,392,000 kilometres from side to side – 109 times wider than the Earth. The Sun is powered by a nuclear reaction. This makes it so hot that it contains only liquid and gases, and releases energy as heat and light.

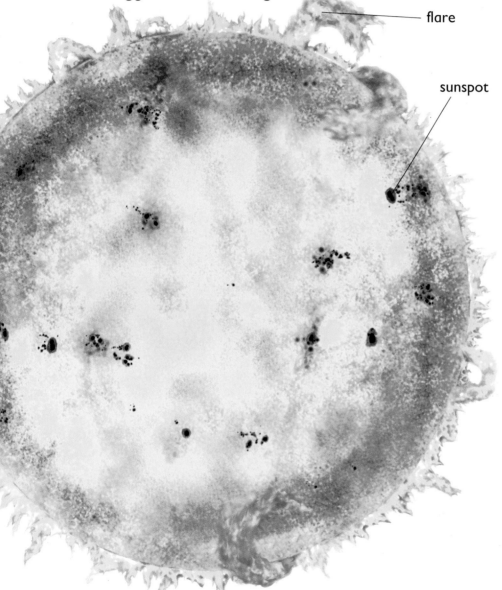

flare

sunspot

Word box

nuclear reaction
process where materials that give off lots of powerful radiation break down to release huge amounts of energy

sunspot
dark patch on the Sun's surface, where great storms break through

▼ Aurora borealis

Storms on the Sun's surface release huge amounts of energy called radiation. When this passes through our upper atmosphere, it sometimes produces flickering lights in the night sky. These are called the aurora borealis (or the aurora australis if you live south of the Equator).

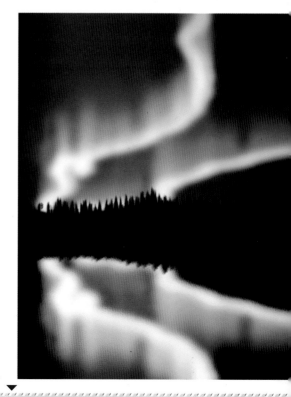

▲ Our stormy Sun

The surface of the Sun is a seething mass of flame. Explosions under the surface produce flares, huge bursts of bright light, that can shoot millions of kilometres into space. When these spectacular events become violent, they are known as solar storms. These can only be seen with special equipment. (Never look directly at the Sun – you could damage your eyes).

Technology

Technology is how we use science to help us.
It began many thousands of years ago, when someone discovered that stones could be broken to make a sharp blade. It has come a long way since then! Today, without technology, we could not travel long distances, surf the Internet or make phone calls to our friends.

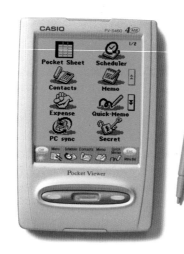

▲ Lazy technology

This is a vacuum cleaner that does all the work by itself! It will wander about the room, cleaning away until it is switched off again. This machine contains sensors that stop it bumping into things or getting stuck in corners.

◄ Pocket PC

Powerful computers can now be packed into pocket-sized devices called Personal Digital Assistants (PDAs). They do not have a normal keyboard, and information is loaded from a large computer, or is keyed in by touching the screen with a small pen called a stylus.

Wow!

Scientists are planning to make tiny machines that can be injected into our bodies! They will be used to repair damaged body tissues. This is called nanotechnology.

► Tiny technology

A tiny chip made from silicon contains the whole 'brain' of a computer, even though it is smaller than a fingernail. The chips do not use much power so they can be built into almost any machine. You will not even know they are there!

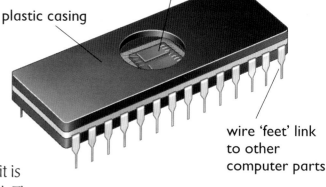

silicon 'wafer'

plastic casing

wire 'feet' link to other computer parts

► Working robots

Computer-controlled robots are used for many jobs, such as making cars and spacecraft. This robotic lifting device, called the Canadarm, was built by the Canadians for use on American space shuttles.

Technology for fun

Find out more:
Computers ◀ Electricity in action ◀
Photography ◀ Technology ◀

Technology costs millions of euros to develop, but sometimes we can use it just for fun! Whole computers can be packed into toys, and some video games use lots of computing power. Once new technology is developed, people work out all sorts of other uses for it, whether you are at home, at school or on the move.

▶ Cyber dog

This robot dog is powered by a battery, and contains a simple computer that controls its movements. It can also understand and act on basic commands.

▲ On the move

Mini discs are tiny versions of the CD. Mini disc players are small and light, so will fit in your pocket. They have a 'skip-free' device, so that the music will not jump when you are moving around. Most allow you to record from CDs.

◀ Computer power

When you play a computer game, you are actually using a very powerful computer. The computer has to make millions of calculations just to make a single object move across the screen.

▲ Movie star

You can make and star in your own movies! Small digital video cameras like this include the software to let you edit your own movie and create special effects. The camera records information on a memory chip. The end result can then be viewed on a computer screen or sent as emails.

Word box

edit
put together material for a film, TV programme, book or newspaper

software
the programs used by a computer

Time

Time can be measured in various ways. You can tell the time roughly by looking at the length of shadows. But the need for accurate time became important, in general, when railways spread around the world in the mid-1800s and train timetables were developed. Now time can be measured even more precisely with atomic clocks, which use decaying radioactive materials.

◀ Sea clocks

Harrison's 'chronometer' was invented by a clock-maker, John Harrison, in the mid-1700s. Powered by a spring, it kept accurate time over long distances. For the first time, it let sailors work out their exact position at sea, so they were less likely to get lost.

▲ Sands of time

An hourglass contains sand in a glass container. The sand runs through a small hole. It was a popular type of clock in the Middle Ages (between the years 470 and 1450), when it was used to measure short periods of time.

▼ Modern times

A digital quartz watch keeps time by using a tiny crystal that vibrates (shakes to and fro) 32,768 times a second when electricity passes through it.

Word box

radioactive
radioactive materials give off powerful radiation (energy). At the same time they 'decay' – change into a different form

▼ Giant calculator

Stonehenge, in England, is a huge circle of stones, thousands of years old. Some astronomers (people who study the stars and planets) believe it was built to tell the time of the seasons by the shadows that the stones cast.

Time around the world

Through the day, time is measured from 12 o'clock midnight. But as the Earth turns, our midnight might be midday on the other side of the world. So we have divided the world into different time zones.

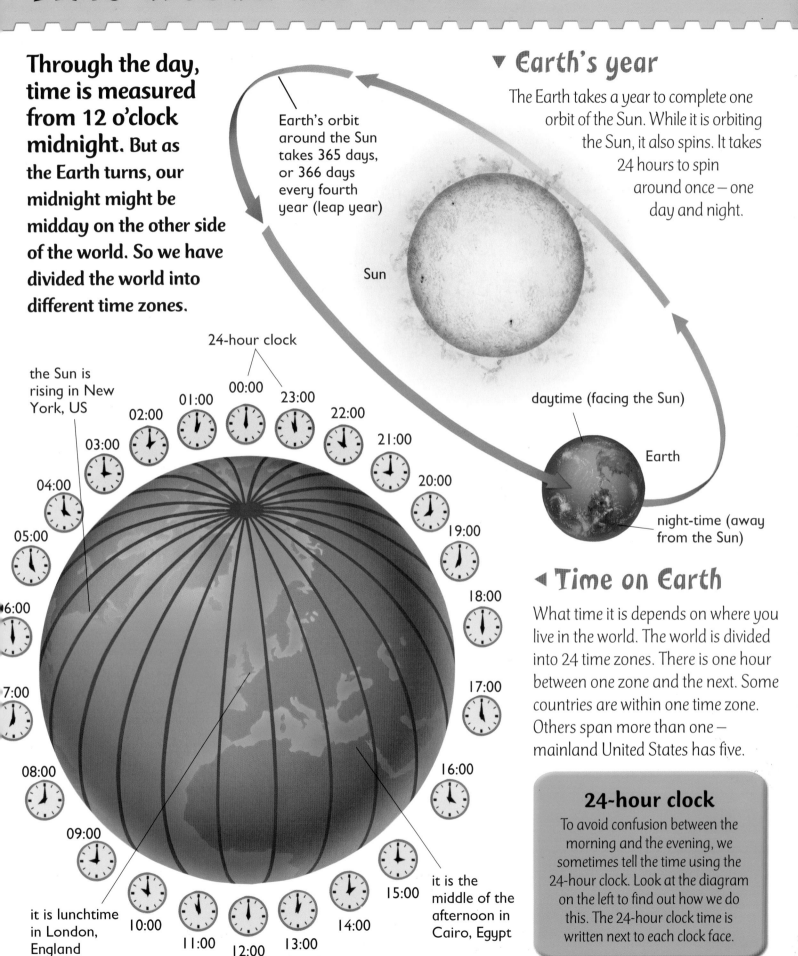

Earth's orbit around the Sun takes 365 days, or 366 days every fourth year (leap year)

Sun

▼ Earth's year

The Earth takes a year to complete one orbit of the Sun. While it is orbiting the Sun, it also spins. It takes 24 hours to spin around once – one day and night.

daytime (facing the Sun)

Earth

night-time (away from the Sun)

24-hour clock

the Sun is rising in New York, US

00:00
01:00
02:00
03:00
04:00
05:00
06:00
07:00
08:00
09:00
10:00
11:00
12:00
13:00
14:00
15:00
16:00
17:00
18:00
19:00
20:00
21:00
22:00
23:00

it is lunchtime in London, England

it is the middle of the afternoon in Cairo, Egypt

◄ Time on Earth

What time it is depends on where you live in the world. The world is divided into 24 time zones. There is one hour between one zone and the next. Some countries are within one time zone. Others span more than one – mainland United States has five.

24-hour clock

To avoid confusion between the morning and the evening, we sometimes tell the time using the 24-hour clock. Look at the diagram on the left to find out how we do this. The 24-hour clock time is written next to each clock face.

Transport on land

Find out more:
Aircraft ◄ Engines ◄ Machines ◄
Transport on water ►

Transport takes people where they want to go, and takes goods from place to place. Land transport is the most common kind of transport. Cars, trains, buses, motocycles and trucks are the main engine-powered means of transport. All of these vehicles ride on wheels.

▲ Power bikes

Motorcycles were developed from the bicycle. They are powered by a petrol engine, and have a much heavier, stronger frame than a bicycle. This is a 1997 Triumph T595 Daytona motorcycle.

► Cleaner cars

Petrol and diesel cars burn up huge amounts of fuel and pollute the atmosphere. Electric cars, like this one, are powered by chemical batteries rather than petrol or diesel oil, and are a cleaner alternative.

► Heavy loads

Most goods are carried by road in trucks. They help transport nearly everything we need in our everyday lives, from food and clothes to the letters we get in the post. Most trucks have more powerful engines than cars, and run mostly on diesel fuel.

◄ Top speed

Some trains now match aeroplanes for speed. France's *TGV* (*Train à Grande Vitesse*, or high-speed train) is one of the world's fastest trains. Normally, it cruises at 300 kilometres per hour, but it has been known to travel up to 500 kilometres per hour.

Transport on water

Find out more:
Aircraft ◄ Engines ◄ Machines in history ◄
Transport on land ◄

The first water transport was developed by prehistoric (early) people, thousands of years ago. They built rafts made of logs or reeds. The development of boats took many centuries. It was not until the 1400s that ships capable of making long ocean voyages were built. Today, high-speed motor boats take us places in no time at all.

▲ Speedy boats

Hydroplanes are motor boats that skim across the surface of the water. They are a cross between a boat and a plane. They have special 'wings' which raise the hull (frame) above the water.

▲ The steam age

The invention of the steam engine during the 1700s opened the way for transport. By the late 1800s, ships powered by steam engines were quickly taking the place of sailing ships.

▲ Getting bigger

During the 1400s, ship-builders began to make ships four times as large as any built before. These ships had a rudder (a piece of wood beneath the back of the ship used for steering) rather than steering oars. Most had three masts and at least three sails.

◄ Wind power

A catamaran is a raft-like boat powered by the wind. It is made of lightweight materials, with two hulls. These allow the boat to slip through the water easily. Some have outriggers (extra floats). These are developed from traditional Polynesian outriggers.

UFOs and aliens

For a long time, many people have thought that life might exist on other planets. Some believe that 'alien' beings have visited us, and that UFOs (Unidentified Flying Objects) are their spaceships. Certain people who believe this have produced blurry pictures to back up what they say. However, there is still no really solid proof.

► Alien craft

For years, humans have imagined what alien craft might look like. No one really knows, as we can't imagine what type of power would let these beings, or aliens, travel freely across space.

► Radio signals

Some scientists study the radio waves that reach us from space, trying to find a signal from other intelligent life. They also send signals into space to try and contact alien life but as the stars are so far away it could take thousands of years before their messages reach anyone.

▼ Flying saucers

Starting in the 1940s, many people have reported seeing saucer-shaped flying objects. They are said to be able to fly at impossibly fast speeds. These flying saucers are supposed to be controlled by aliens, but there is no real evidence for this.

Universe

The Universe contains everything that exists.
This includes the Earth, other planets, and billions of stars. The Universe is about 15,000 million years old – and still growing. Scientists believe it was probably born after a very large explosion which they call the Big Bang.

Word box

elliptical
egg-shaped

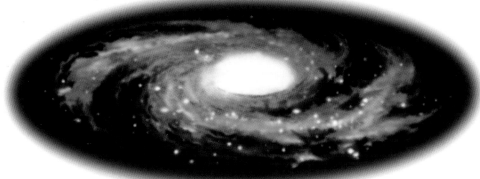

▼ Galaxy clusters

Out in space there are glowing clouds made up of masses of floating dust. These are called nebulas, and they often look like smudges of light. Nebulas also contain millions of stars. Nebulas and stars form huge clusters called galaxies. Our own galaxy is called the Milky Way.

▲ Cosmic rays

Stars produce huge amounts of energy. This reaches the Earth as heat, light and cosmic rays, made of tiny particles (objects). These particles travel so fast that when they hit other particles in our atmosphere they smash them, releasing bursts of radiation energy.

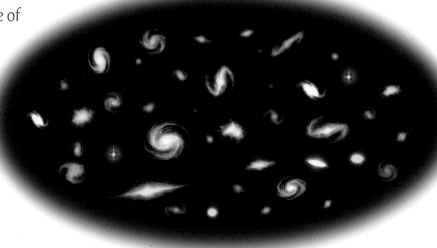

▼ Spins and streamers

Galaxies come in different shapes. Many of them are spinning. The stars they contain trail out to form long streamers.

spiral galaxy	irregular galaxy	elliptical galaxy	spiral galaxy with bar across

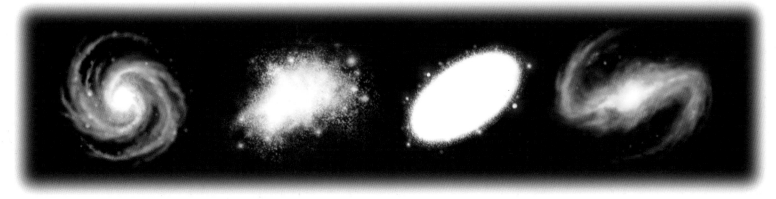

Water

Water has shaped our world. It has gradually worn down rocks and produced the soil in which plants grow. No animals or plants could survive without some water to drink. Frozen water forms the great icecaps at the North and South Poles. Most of the world's water is in the oceans, and is salty. Fresh water, with no salt, is found in rivers and lakes.

How much rain?

Use a jam jar to measure rainfall. Place the jar where the rain can fall into it. Use a marker pen to mark the water level on the outside of the jar. Keep a record of the changing levels in a notebook.

▲ Frozen drips

Icicles form when snow or ice melts and then re-freezes. The snow starts to melt during the day. Then the dripping water freezes again in the colder night temperatures.

▼ The water cycle

The water cycle involves all the water on Earth. Water droplets or vapours rise from lakes, rivers and seas to form clouds. These droplets join up to make bigger drops that eventually fall as rain. Some rain is soaked up by the land. Much of it runs back to the sea.

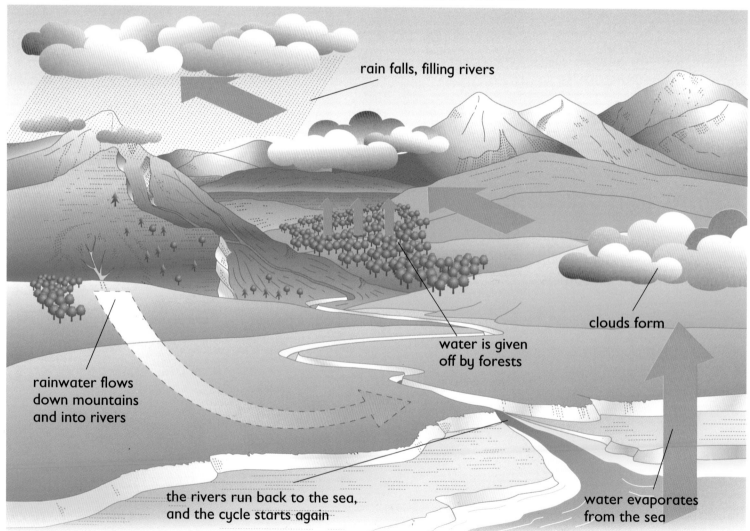

rain falls, filling rivers

water is given off by forests

clouds form

rainwater flows down mountains and into rivers

the rivers run back to the sea, and the cycle starts again

water evaporates from the sea

Water and life

Find out more:
Oceans and seas ◀ Plant kingdom ◀ Plant life ◀
Water ◀

All life depends on water. Our cells are made mostly from water. We carry lots of water in our blood. Like most animals, our bodies are usually able to stop us from losing too much water. But as we cannot store water, we still need to drink very regularly. Making sure that people have germ-free drinking water is vital for good health.

◀ Pot plants

Plants in pots can't get water from the ground, so they need regular watering. Too little water means they die. Too much can also kill them, by rotting their roots.

▶ Water holes

Oases are the few places in deserts that have water under the surface of the sand. Rainwater sinks into the sand, then collects in rock. The water moves through the rock to form a pool where the land dips down. Plants and animals can survive there.

oasis

rock

water beneath rock

▼ Life in a rock pool

Rock pools contain lots of different plants and animals. All of them are adapted to withstand pounding waves and hot sun in the shallow water. Rock pools give you an idea of the huge variety of life in the sea.

hermit crabs have no shell, so 'borrow' a leftover one from another sea creature

razorshell

limpets

snail

mussel

anemone

sea urchin

blenny

sponges are animals that filter food from sea water

starfish are relatives of sea urchins and sea cucumbers

shore crabs are very hardy

seaweeds take in nutrients (goodness) from water

Weather

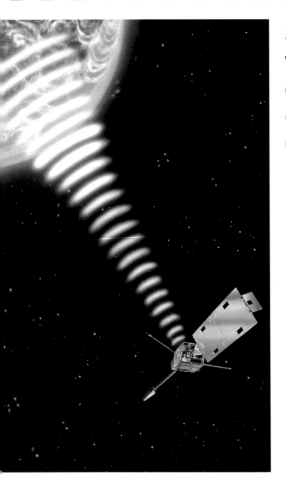

Sun, wind and water combine to produce our weather. The Sun's heat makes water from the sea evaporate (turns it into tiny droplets). These droplets rise and form clouds in the cooler upper atmosphere. Clouds are carried by the wind and deposit rain over the land.

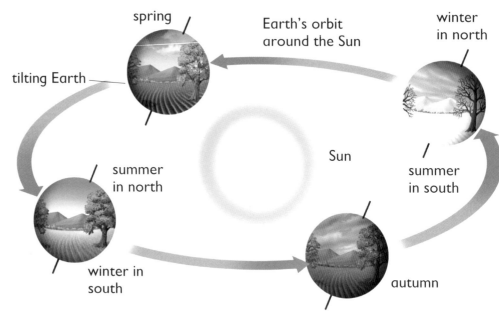

spring
Earth's orbit around the Sun
winter in north
tilting Earth
Sun
summer in north
summer in south
winter in south
autumn

▲ Sent by satellite

Clouds and storms gathering above the Earth can be seen clearly from space. Satellites photograph them and send radio messages back to Earth. The movement of the storms and clouds allows scientists to predict (guess) what the weather will be like.

▶ Cloud shapes

Clouds form at different heights, and in different types of weather. These things affect their appearance. Generally, the thin, wispy clouds are high up. Heavy-looking rain clouds are normally nearer the ground.

Word box

evaporate
turn into tiny droplets

satellite
a spacecraft travelling around Earth

▲ The seasons

Weather varies with the seasons. These happen as the Earth circles the Sun. One full circle takes a year. The Earth is tilted, so the poles get closer to the Sun at different times. In June, the North Pole leans towards the Sun, making it summer in northern areas.

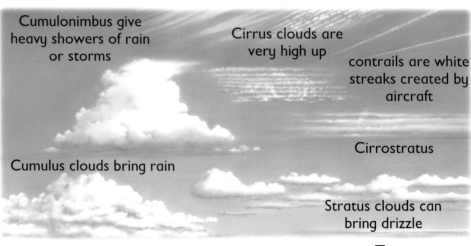

Cumulonimbus give heavy showers of rain or storms

Cirrus clouds are very high up

contrails are white streaks created by aircraft

Cirrostratus

Cumulus clouds bring rain

Stratus clouds can bring drizzle

X-rays

The invention of the X-ray machine meant doctors could see exactly what was going on inside a living body. There are now many other types of body-scanner. They 'see' inside the body by using sound waves and other forms of energy that are able to pass through living tissue.

▲ Airport security

To make sure that people do not carry anything dangerous on board an aircraft, their baggage is X-rayed. An X-ray can travel through most soft substances but not hard ones. This means that even the smallest objects can be seen inside a case.

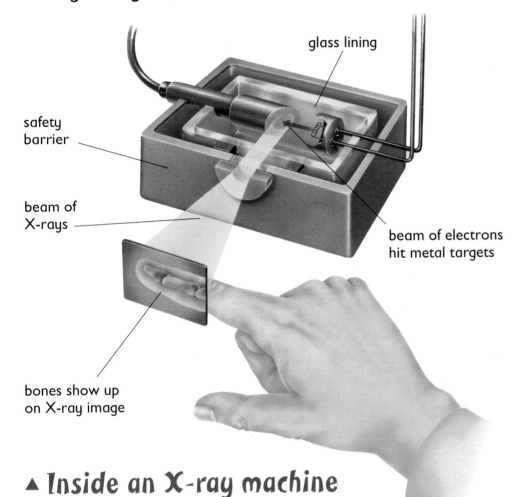

glass lining

safety barrier

beam of X-rays

beam of electrons hit metal targets

bones show up on X-ray image

▲ Inside an X-ray machine

X-rays are produced in a glass discharge tube. They pass through the body and make an image on a screen or on photographic film. As bone is harder than flesh, it leaves a shadow that can be seen very clearly.

▶ Dental X-rays

Your dentist may X-ray your teeth to find out what is happening inside a tooth. Any infection and cavities (holes) show up on the X-ray pictures, so the dentist knows what treatment to give you.

Word box

discharge tube
vacuum-filled (without air) glass tube through which electricity is passed

electron
a tiny particle

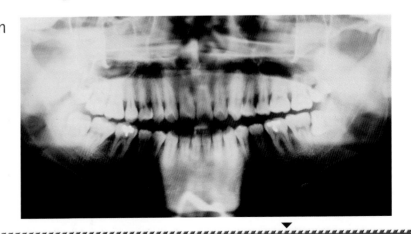

Index

The numbers in **bold** type refer to main entries in your book

**The publishers would like to thank
the following artists who have contributed
to this book:**

Mark Bergin, Steve Caldwell, Kuo Kang Chen,
Mark Davis/Mackerel, Peter Dennis, Richard Draper,
Nicholas Forder, Chris Forsey, Mike Foster/Maltings
Partnership, Mark Franklin, Terry Gabbey,
Studio Galante, Shammi Ghale, Alan Hancocks,
Peter Harper, Alan Harris, Kevin Maddison, Alan Male,
Janos Marffy, Helen Parsley, Terry Riley, Steve Roberts,
Martin Sanders, Mike Saunders, Gwen Tourret,
Steve Weston, Tony Wilkins, Rudi Vizi

**The publishers would like to thank
the following for supplying photographs
for this book:**

Casio: 66 (b/r); 82 (c)
Corbis: Gary Bartholemew 31 (t/r);
Jacques M. Chenet 93 (b/r); Digital Art 88 (b);
Owen Franken 62 (b/l); Michael Gore, Frank Lane
Picture Agency 25 (b/r); Paul A. Souders 31 (t/l);
Lawson Wood 21 (b/l)
**Corel, digitalSTOCK, digitalvision,
Electrolux:** 82 (c/l), **John Foxx, Hemera,
IntelPlay:** 83 (b/l), **Nokia:** 23 (t/l),
**PhotoEssentials,
PhotoPROc, Sony:** 83 (t/l)

All other pictures from the MKP Archives